Miguel Ángel García Morc'''

EDUCATION IS A MATTER OF THE HEART

The Educational-Pastoral Model of The Salesians of Don Bosco

Don Bosco Publications

Don Bosco Publications
Thornleigh House, Sharples Park, Bolton BL1 6PQ
United Kingdom

ISBN 978-1-909080-84-3
©Don Bosco Publications 2022
© Miguel Ángel García Morcuende SDB

The moral rights of the author have been asserted

Original Spanish title: *La Educación Es Cosa De Corazones*, @2017, PPC,
Madrid

Italian: *L'educazione è cosa di cuori*, @2019, Editrice Elledici, Turin

English translation with permission from the author

Front cover: Marek Studzinski/Unsplash

Illustrations: Agustín de la Torre Zarazaga Design

Printed in the UK by Jump DP

FSC
www.fsc.org

MIX
Paper from
responsible sources
FSC® C004309

To educate is an act of love, it is to give life.
And love is demanding, it calls for the best resources,
for a reawakening of the passion to begin this path
patiently with young people.

Pope Francis
Clementine Hall
Thursday, February 13, 2014

Contents

Foreword

The turbulence of the nineteenth century in Italy is the context of the foundation of the Salesian work of St John Bosco, familiarly known as Don Bosco. The Salesian charism, his educational method and his spirituality translate into a persistent concern for the most vulnerable adolescents and young people. His manifold experience in works and initiatives is still very relevant today in the field of education; many of his intuitions are still extremely relevant, even when one considers the time in which they were proposed to the young people and educators of his time. The history of Don Bosco the educator, viewed in some of its most significant milestones, helps us to understand some of the constants and some of the most distinctive features of the identity, historical tradition and transforming dynamics of the Salesian way of educating. As a committed educator, a fruitful evangeliser, a catechetical practitioner and an inexhaustible writer, he was committed from the beginning to seek out abandoned, scattered and needy young people in order to gather them together and give them the means of subsistence: work, education and hope for a better tomorrow. Don Bosco embodies in his own person, that programme which he enunciated many times: "We are in times when we must act"; we must "work, and work tirelessly, if we do not want to witness the total ruin of this generation"; it is necessary to "unite around what has to be done and act".

Thus, he opened his Oratory in 1844, dedicating it to St Francis de Sales, and in 1846, he succeeded in giving it a permanent home. He was a young man who lived in a house on the outskirts of Turin, in the area called Valdocco. His sole aim was to set in motion a great movement of people for the moral, psychological, spiritual and physical benefit of those young people. His providential presence has given meaning to the personal history of many more young people, has given it meaning and therefore made it beautiful.

Signs from above, natural aptitudes, the advice of discreet people, personal discernment and providential opportunities convinced him that God was calling him to a total dedication to young people: "It is enough that you are young for me to love you with all my soul," he said in the introduction to his book '*Il giovane provveduto*' (The Companion of Youth).[1] Today there are many generations of young people and Salesian educators under this attentive gaze.

In these pages we will see clearly how all his life he, a dreamer, was a builder of ideals and a sower of hope, concerned about the fate of the poorest children and adolescents. His most important dreams were sown in the hearts of many generous people, and today his is a living charism in the most remote and needy corners of 132 countries.

We are pleased to present a text in which Fr Miguel Ángel intends to expound this great educational and pastoral movement that is linked to the figure of Don Bosco; not only did the Turin saint lay out a set of pedagogical inspirations, but he is also heir to an educational praxis which he calls, in a general and holistic way, the 'Preventive System'. Education was the heart and soul of his practical and conceptual programme, while his system—as an ideal and concrete collection of convictions and procedures—was the model through which he expressed it. The booklet entitled *The Preventive system in the Education of the Young* (1877) is considered to be, not without good reason, the compendium of Don Bosco's pedagogical ideas. In reality, it represents Salesian education.

Throughout the text, the basic principles of his educational system are presented in a conceptual way, with accurate observations on its origins and on the profile of the educators vis-à-vis the young people, the educational institutions and the methods used.

Within this geographical and organisational diversity of the Salesians in the world, the educational-pastoral model invites us to face new scenarios and,

---

1   G. Bosco, *The Companion of Youth for the Practice of Religious Duties*, online: https://www.sdb.org/en/Don_Bosco/Writings/Writings/The_Companion_of_Youth_for_the_Practice_of_Religious_Duties_ [Accessed 29/06/2022].

consequently, new challenges in order to approach and respond to a society immersed in the twenty-first century from the charism and the Gospel. These efforts are expressed in abundant documents and educational reference texts, with the aim of adapting to reality, reformulating and updating their scope of action. The Second Vatican Council obliged the Salesians to begin a long process of reflection, drawing from the sources of the great conciliar constitutions. From the immediate post-conciliar period they committed themselves professionally to read the signs of the times and to respond with generosity and creativity to new needs and new urgencies. In this way, the educational-pastoral proposal has been nourished and renewed in the light of Synodal paths, with their Apostolic Exhortations, alongside the magisterium of the Church.

This path of reflection and action has found solid and clear support in the *Constitutions and Regulations of the Society of Francis de Sales* (1984) and in the General Chapters of the Salesians from 1965 (GC 19) to 2014 (GC 27), which have marked a path of renewal and reflection on educational and pastoral practice. Also in the magisterium of the Rector Majors, who have offered their uninterrupted and prophetic reflection and have wisely guided this process of evangelisation and education.

In this way, rethinking all of this heritage, Fr Miguel Ángel offers here an updated reflection on the Preventive System of Don Bosco. He has also wanted to build on the idea of the educational-pastoral community, as a clear vision of a project that defines the evangelising and educational identity of every type of Salesian presence (and Salesian educational-pastoral project). It shows how the educational-pastoral model is also bound up with proposing Salesian youth spirituality, experienced by a broad movement of people.

For this reason, we want to emphasise the strongly idealistic character of the text and the conviction that it can contribute in two ways: on the one hand, to spread a better historical, spiritual and pedagogical knowledge of the Salesian educational-pastoral model; on the other, to renew the commitment to generously giving to such a beautiful and important cause as accompanying the young people of the twenty-first century.

Fabio Attard, SDB
General Councillor for Salesian Youth Ministry, 2021

Introduction

Every reflection begins with a title. The heading of any book is already an indication, it is not selected by chance; it is a choice among other possibilities. We propose to make known, or to interiorise, the Salesian educational-pastoral model, animated by the social, educational and spiritual legacy of Don Bosco. In this case it is a modest and incomplete contribution, however, both aspects of which do not detract from the novelty and the original freshness of the project.

1. We have chosen to speak of an *educational-pastoral model,* because we understand that any 'educational' system oriented to the formation of new generations is a paradigm; that is, it contains a set of theoretical and historical elements that determine its way of being and acting in an educational institution, its practical pedagogy, its traditions, its language, its symbols, its approaches and other explicit and implicit elements that provide it with its own identity. But the model is also defined as 'pastoral' in its purpose, content and style. It holds in tension an ideal of society and of humankind, its meaning, its destiny and its import. Therefore, our perspective excludes in fact any dissociation between education and evangelisation.

Thus, we intend to affirm that Salesian youth ministry is characterised by its educational modality, and that Salesian pedagogy is distinguished by its constant pastoral purpose. In this sense, we will have to elucidate on the essential elements of this educational and evangelising approach to clarify its anthropological, theological, pedagogical, methodological and pastoral stance.

This means that we will ask ourselves the relevant anthropological and theological questions: what kind of person and society do we want to foster? What ideal values are behind the concept of the human being? What is education for? In analogous terms, we will scrutinise this from a pastoral perspective: how do we understand the intentionality of evangelisation? What educational conditions should be in place?

In these pages we want to focus on the educational task and the very purpose of education. We will not go into questions of how to conceive the practice of academic educational processes, i.e., the most appropriate teaching models for the meaningful assimilation of knowledge, skills and values, didactic applications, curriculum or assessment of learning. The task will not be the development of these teaching and learning processes, which, although formulated on the basis of the purpose of education as set out in the educational model, is more concerned with the didactic area of school and vocational training.

Knowledge of the Salesian educational model will allow educators and the entire educational-pastoral community to have an overview of how to operate and what the elements are that play a determining role in any Salesian presence, especially with the most needy, abandoned, denied and oppressed young people. In truth, young people today are living in exciting times, surrounded by a context full of challenges and possibilities. It is also full of personal subjectivities, microcosms rich in dreams, small universes that the educator must know and appreciate. The Salesian educator, to whom these pages are addressed, must be aware and appreciate how to accompany the new generations in a society that does not know how to tune into the deepest desires of young people, who demand not only creative, enterprising and competent accompaniers, but also those with high relational and witnessing skills.

2. Secondly, in fidelity to the title of the book, we will focus on the educational experience of Don Bosco, the fruit of his personal journey and of his educational endeavour. The Salesian educational-pastoral model cannot be understood today if we do not place it within the scope of the Preventive System of Don Bosco or, more concretely, in its praxis and its institutional consistency. It is here that it acquires its organic meaning. Born in an all-embracing educational environment and conducive to an 'integral education',

the Oratory of Valdocco was a formative space that allowed a unique family coexistence of educators and students in every moment of daily life.

This institution was not new in the Italian catechetical and educational tradition; in fact, it had begun in the sixteenth century with St Philip Neri and St Charles Borromeo. But at Don Bosco it is a meeting place for educators and young people, a family in an educational environment of freedom and commitment in which the affection shown becomes a human means of attraction and achievement. All this is reinforced through an organisation of initiatives of all kinds.

In fact, for the great majority of these young people, the educational services and the institutions designed for them were an unexpected gift, an opportunity, a wonderful possibility of life and the beginning of a new path.

3. Gradually, we will try to visualise today the identity of the model, its educational ideal, its particularly apostolic character, its formative priorities, its pedagogical interventions at a personal, group or environmental level. It is thus a source of inspiration for the planning and development of educational projects, structures and activities. Some may be of an extraordinary nature, but most tend to be consistent over time and rely on courageous, thoughtful and well-planned projects.

To make this journey possible, we are going to explore two pathways that will help us to enter into the Salesian educational-pastoral model: a historical-foundational one and a more operative one. Both pathways illuminate and enrich each other. The two perspectives are interwoven throughout this book.

The first is fundamentally descriptive (theoretical framework) and therefore focuses on the *raison d'être* of the model, the substance of the main intentions. The first three chapters correspond to this first chapter:

—The first establishes the meaning and purposes of the Salesian educational-pastoral model; by presenting a specific mission, its vision of the future is reported and the values with which it intends to work are set out.

—This is followed by a discussion of the originality—the origin—of the educational-pastoral model in its first institutions and services (Chapter Two), in a continuous dialectic between ideal and reality, between intentions and concrete situations, between principles and circumstances; the chapter will also look at Don Bosco's biographical experience and the most significant moments of his work.

—Finally, the beliefs that inspire and guide the Salesian educational-pastoral approach contained in the Preventive System (Chapter Three) are presented as an integrated educational project (pastoral), as a spirituality that supports living a Christian life and, finally, as a practical pedagogical method (this aspect will be taken up again in Chapter Six).

The second part or pathway has been organised around four chapters, as follows:

—The trinomial 'reason, religion, kindness' constitutes the physiognomy of the Preventive System, which needs to be structured within the educational-pastoral community in order to be implemented. This is our focus in Chapter Four, responding to the question of who we are and why we are all important; in addition, we will describe the identity of the educator as a person, as a professional, as a Christian and as a promoter of a Salesian educational and evangelising project.

—Since the model needs to be operative, we will ground it in the educational-pastoral project, which is an instrument for a better interpretation of the reality of the Salesian approach. The formative programme of the model is set out in Chapter Five. Here we will start from a firm conviction: at the basis of every educational model there is always a model of the person to which we aspire, an anthropological horizon, a pre-understanding within which it develops and is justified. We propose from this perspective that a determined educational orientation derives from each concept of the person: education is not indifferent to this dimension.

—The pedagogical and pastoral indications, the 'how to' of the Salesian style, are found in Chapter Six. This educational 'good practice' is proposed under an iconography typical of the Salesian tradition: a 'house' that welcomes, a home for living, a family where everyone feels accompanied; a 'parish' that evangelises in a climate of values, ethics and Christian commitment; a 'school' in which harmonious development and the potential of each person is fostered; the 'playground' as an environment that favours and develops the meeting and the celebration.

If in the first three chapters, reference is made to the 'idea' of the Salesian model and the reasons that started it, Chapters Four to Six refer to the 'method'. Now we need to stop at the 'action', that is, to get fully involved in the structures where the approach is developed. From this thinking, we will arrive at the description of institutions and services (Chapter Seven), in which we highlight elements of congruence between the model and daily life in these various Salesian educational-pastoral environments.

At the end, an epilogue tries to highlight some challenges which translate into specific recommendations. It is not possible to maintain an educational-pastoral approach by repeating the same practices or even by indulging in complacency; it is not possible to reject or fear change. Salesian institutions have to face the twenty-first century creatively in order to bring educational and pastoral innovation and renew their critical and hopeful outlook.

4. Finally, we should note the valuable contribution of the 'Salesian Youth Ministry: Frame of Reference'[1] to the drafting of this text. The publication of this organic synthesis, which was very positively received in all contexts, presents itself as a rich overview of the Salesian educational-pastoral heritage in response to modern challenges.

This text, which we continually draw on in these pages, can be represented by a metaphor: the famous Rubik's cube, that geometrical puzzle that organises, in a rather exhaustive way, all the facets of Salesian youth ministry, arranging them in various ways, giving rise to so many possible combinations.

With this visual picture in mind, it can be asserted that the presentation of the Salesian model is not limited to a description of the elements of a proposal crystallised over time; it also provides a useful representation of the potential it has for educational and pastoral practices.

---

1   Salesian Youth Ministry Department, *Salesian Youth Ministry: Frame of Reference*, [3rd ed.], (Rome: Direzione Generale Opere Don Bosco, 2014).

Chapter One

The Meaning and Purpose of the Salesian Educational-Pastoral Model

1. A Salesian Model: "why?" and "what for?"

In order to define the identity of an educational model in an institution, it is important to reflect on the following set of questions: Who are we? What do we seek? Where do we want to go? In other words, the what, the how and the why of an educational paradigm. These are fundamental questions that challenge every educator, the answers to which should never be taken for granted.

As we said in the introduction, the relationship between pedagogical ideas and educational practice is mediated by an 'educational model'; a frame of reference that explains the positioning of the human being and his or her ability to learn, on which the educational project and each institution are based. It is a point of arrival and a point of departure, a bridge between the philosophy, the values, the principles of an institution and its daily educational practice.

On the one hand, by focusing on the concept of the person to be formed in all its dimensions, this broad and dynamic model of reference directs its attention towards the profile of the educator who should be the source of inspiration for educational action. It must also set out the educational project that is proposed and the particular educational style that it promotes. Moreover, if all education is seen as a community process, enriched by many agents, it should also specify who will participate in the creation of that context of belonging or educational community.

1. The experience of St John Bosco in the Oratory, the pedagogical space par excellence for our study, provides a particular way of understanding the originality of the Salesian way. It is essential to recognise that Don Bosco's educational concern is situated within a process of humanisation that promotes the integral growth of the young person, especially in an urban environment.[1] An almost utopian project not only of intellectual, professional, physical or moral growth of the young people of the working classes and those at risk, but also a proposal for religious growth.

It is not so much a matter of copying this experience as of creatively developing the originality of those rich intuitions and operative proposals with historical relevance. Only in this way is the model able to stand up credibly to the demands of the current culture and to be measured against the educational challenges of today.

2. It is true that Don Bosco is part of a group of religious men and women who, during the period of modern and contemporary history, have founded educational institutions; however, in him the strong link between education and the holiness of youth is presented with greater consistency as a particular

---

1   The study of P. Braido, *La experiencia pedagógica de Don Bosco.* (Rome: LAS, 1988), offers a complete vision, with abundant documentation and with the rigour and competence of this well-known and authoritative scholar of Don Bosco's pedagogy. It is a work of continuous reference in our study.

trait that we will see in Chapter Three. Neither education nor holiness are new, what is new is the nature and extent of the relationship between them and how they come together to form the young anew.[2] It can be said that the originality and audacity of Don Bosco's educational art always sought points of interchange, common places where Christian humanism and educational processes came together.

Educational and evangelising initiatives find a harmonious place within the origins and environment of the Salesian Oratory. For this reason, the frame of reference which we present in these pages invites young people to discover their life project, always in close correlation with the commitment to transform the world according to God's plan for each one of them.

In summary, we can define the Salesian proposal as an educational-pastoral model, because the goal is the construction of the individual personality in light of Christian anthropology; an educational ideal which, by making itself explicit and interactive, is capable of forming those new young people that society demands.

3. Don Bosco's educational experience transcends what he had thought, structured and applied. His project meets the needs and expectations of today's generations. In fact, the Salesians of Don Bosco, as a formative institution, have been undergoing a profound process of rethinking, seeking to strengthen their identity and their position. They have been obliged to outline possible, viable and significant educational-pastoral goals for the young people of today, always based on a clearly educational and evangelising approach. This can be seen in the presence of more organised and more traditional structures, such as the oratory-youth centre, the school and the vocational training centre,

---

2   The Salesian theologian and moralist Xavier Thévenot tried to enculturate the Preventive System to make it attractive and relevant in the present century, always within the framework of educational accompaniment. His thesis is centred on this statement: the educational relationship is a form of holiness. A new form of educational presence is the privileged space for the experience of God. It is based on a strong investment in the learner-educator relationship, in their respective capacities: the capacity for resilience on the one hand, adaptation and listening on the other (cf. Th. Le Goaziou, 'Il senso della relazione educativa secondo Xavier Thévenot, moralista salesiano (1938-2004)', in V. Orlando [ed.], Con Don Bosco, educatori dei giovani del nostro tempo. Atti del Convegno Internazionale di Pedagogia Salesiana, 19-21 March 2015, Rome, Salesianum/ UPS (Rome: LAS, 2015), 341–43).

the Salesian presence in higher education, the parish-community and social services for young people at risk.

Having said this, it should also be noted that there are other structures and services which try to respond to these new challenges. We are referring to the centres of vocational animation, the specialised services of Christian formation and spiritual animation, the associations and services of animation in the field of leisure (sport, tourism, etc.), and the services of animation in the field of the apostolate. These sectors will be discussed in Chapter Seven.

2. The Purpose and Framework of the Educational Pastoral Model

2.1. Graphical representation

The educational-pastoral model is defined and articulated around certain goals. To express them visually, we can use the image of the galaxy. We have chosen this image of the planetary system in which everything revolves around a central nucleus; in this case, the world of young people, in whose life and culture we are called to live as educators. A model without a motive or orientation loses its *raison d'être*. Therefore, the force or imperative that drives this movement is pastoral charity, the "centre and synthesis"[3] of the Salesian spirit. This visual and dynamic form is drawn precisely to express that it is a living process much more than a rigid structure of principles; it is an organic reality whose elements are mutually interrelated in continuous movement.

Within this galaxy, multiple elements can be found which revolve themselves and also in relation to all the others, forming areas of contact and mutual interaction. In fact, the successful educational-pastoral model requires theological and anthropological criteria for reading and interpreting in order to understand the Good News and respond to the needs of young people in a relevant way; on the other hand, the model has before it the first task or purpose: to meet Jesus and profess him as Lord of one's own life, with education being the place and the mediation (to evangelise and to educate). The graphic representation with these two aspects breaks the vicious circle

---

3   In these terms it is expressed in article 21 of the *Constitutions of the Salesians of Don Bosco* (ed. 1984).

of an educational-pastoral action that simply 'does' and of a pedagogy that 'thinks', in order to introduce the virtuous circle of an educational action that is 'wise' in its practice and of a pedagogy that 'serves it through thought'.

The dynamic understanding of this system needs to make this dynamism applicable in a Salesian way, i.e., some particular basic choices. Thus, 'the Salesian galaxy' requires a charismatic inspiration, a "spiritual and educational experience": the *Preventive System.*[4] It also needs a subject or protagonist, the *educational-pastoral community,* oriented to create a consensus in the world of youth from all possible points of view. To all this is added an orientation of a method, an operative instrument: the *educational-pastoral project.*

Finally, a distinct operational form must be represented in the vision of this model, i.e. the structures, processes and styles of animation and coordination. All this is embodied in activities, works, services, planning and distribution of figures, functions and participatory bodies.

---

4   This is the definition of the Preventive System in article 20 of the *Constitutions of the Salesians of Don Bosco* (ed. 1984).

2.2. The educational option from a faith perspective

> Don Bosco educates and evangelises by carrying out a project that promotes personal integration. He considered education in its broad and comprehensive meaning: as the growth of the person and as a set of necessary interventions available for each person. Evangelisation inspires and illuminates the fullness of life offered in Jesus, respecting the evolving circumstances of young people, especially the poorest, for whom and in whom culture is humanised and evangelised.

Here we find, by way of a frame of reference, a specific position on the concept of evangelisation, human beings and their ability to learn. This section proposes to offer not so much new reflections as a better conceptualisation of the profound and inseparable relationship between educational and evangelising action. Few terms like 'education' and 'evangelisation' have such expressive and complementary links for the formation of new generations. Their mutual encounters and disagreements have relevant consequences for the principles and practices of the Salesian educational-pastoral model.

In fact, they are two different processes, neither of which is limited to the other. Educating and evangelising are the ultimate goals of the model, even though they have different logical structures and modes of communication. The first has a very rich lexical ambiguity and refers to the area of the production and communication of culture; it is concerned with the development of the person in a values-based society, with models and life choices, with the balanced management of knowledge and skills; the second is aimed at the explicit presentation of the Gospel to arouse the acceptance of the person and to promote a sense of belonging. In this sense, the communicative structure of evangelisation is the witness to and the confession of faith.

However, we can say that there are points of convergence and balance. Those who evangelise by educating are those who are aware of the intrinsic educational quality of the Gospel proclamation and promote it while presenting the Gospel; and those who, recognising the evangelising purpose of educational action, remain faithful to it while educating. This mutual relationship is not always obvious and, if it is noticed, it is frequently neglected. We will briefly approach each of them in the following reflections.

—Education: a privileged intervention available for people

In new knowledge-based societies, education is seen as the main tool for the personal, social, cultural, economic, political and scientific development of people. The prosperity of a society is reflected in its vision of 'training' in practical terms, in its education policies. This is, in part, the reason why attention to education is prioritised in many countries and international organisations.

We would like to insist at the beginning of this reflection that education is an extraordinary cultural mediation, or rather we could say: education is the main and essential task of culture, of all culture. In fact, the development of societies requires that children, young people and adults be equipped with the knowledge, skills, attitudes and values necessary to improve quality of life and to continue building culture. If, therefore, education is at the service of people, the option of thinking of education not only as an area or a sector, but as an essential dimension of evangelising action for the educational institutions of the Church, is becoming more and more urgent.

1. As we have seen above, by taking a young person in hand, the Salesian proposal accompanies and educates in a broad sense their reasons for living and, through them, their growth. It is an educational process, a creative task of humanisation. That is to say, inviting all the aspects of the person (cognitive, affective, emotional, intuitive, artistic, social, spiritual or ethical) to converse wisely. We speak of a process of humanisation because it places the person at the centre of the educational process as the point of importance and, depending on him or her, the world surrounding them. The aim of education is, on the one hand, to be aware that each person is unique and that their vocation belongs to them; on the other hand, to help each person to develop the capacity to realise it, informing their being and history with humanity.

Education has an intentional nature in that it sets in motion all the potentials of the young person; it is a privileged way of promoting the inner world: to educate is to help to discover oneself and to fulfil oneself as a person; it is to teach how to live, to judge, to evaluate, to act according to the truth and the importance of good; it is to travel from the surface to the foundation; in other words, it is to focus on depth. When we educate a person, we try to give them a profound vision of the world, of themselves and of history. The educator wants the young person to make an introspective journey, to feel the desire to delve into the essence of things and, in particular, into the depths of themselves.

It is not a matter of 're-inventing the person', but of exploring with attention and care, like a gold digger extracting the precious metal that has been hidden in time. For this reason, education is not just a mere one-way transmission of knowledge, but a practice of unveiling, a dynamism that seeks to awaken in the learner the desire to know more, to love more, to be more.

This process implies that all education should have as its conclusion the human fulfilment, the full and integral development of each person, a humanising interest beyond a simple exercise of domestication. For this reason, in this arduous task we can define education as a 'hybrid entity' that is both art and science, intuition and rational thought, artisanal imagination and systematic processes.

But in this argument, we come up against a crucial question for education: what is the integrity of this approach? In today's educational panorama, the concept of 'holistic education' is understood in many different ways. In many cases it is translated as the harmonious and balanced development of the abilities or competencies of the person. In the Salesian educational-pastoral model, it does not indicate the desire to engage and help the young person to integrate all the active psychological and spiritual forces that unify them. In contrast to Marcuse's "one-dimensional man"[5] there is a humanistic, multi-dimensional conception, where the human being is a being of possibilities. And within this concept of wholeness, what role does the religious question play: is it possible to cultivate a holistic approach without this aspect?

2. The first anthropological insight consists in seeing the human being as an open book, as a possibility of self-transcendence, going far beyond themselves, beyond all that they are, beyond all that they have already achieved. If a person is attentive to their own search, they will realise that there is always a deep aspiration that they want to achieve, something that they cannot find within

---

5   H. Marcuse, *One-Dimensional Man: Studies in the Ideology of Advanced Industrial Society*, (Boston: Beacon Press, 1964). Philosopher Herbert Marcuse introduces the concept of the "one dimensional man" as someone who is subjected to a new kind of totalitarianism in the form of consumerist and technological capitalism.

themselves, beyond the surface of the immediate and pressing. Other motives, perspectives and points of reference are needed; it is the human being's openness to the whole of reality.

Today it is inconceivable to understand 'holistic education' without a process of personal identification in which the religious universe is present. An educational service that looks with integrity at the entire formation of young people is not afraid to help them open their eyes, minds and hearts to ultimate questions. The teaching of the religious question is situated here as the formative process by which the person, with the help of educational interventions, assimilates and lives this desire for the transcendent.[6] A professionally coherent formation seeks to be anthropologically significant; it needs to elucidate the knowledge and experience of the transcendent. This obliges us to deepen the anthropological and the theological aspects at the same time.

In the Salesian educational-pastoral praxis we find ourselves faced with a spirituality whose meaning is linked 'together with' and 'in relation to' other questions concerning the meaning of life, the experience of the limitations of the human condition, the aspiration to happiness. All these questions are about the future, about the construction of possible meanings. In their own way, our young people narrate what they want to become, they make the effort to describe different horizons. In their intense stories we find a thirst for spirituality, a thirst for experiences, a thirst for meaning, a thirst for what is essential, a thirst for God. The religious question increases the search and the desire to shape a better future.

The religious question, in the form of faith and belief, is not a transient dimension but is integral to the very being of the person, a legitimate and

---

6   Prof. Martin Lechner, who was director of the Salesian Youth Pastoral Institute in Benediktbeuern, develops the concept of 'education sensitive to religion', which is based on a number of concepts. The first step is to perceive and appreciate the life and religiosity of young people, even those who do not belong to any religious community. Only then can one draw—implicitly through loving education and explicitly through religious education—the attention of young people to faith as the basis for a good life. Cf. M. Lechner, 'L'attenzione alle religione nell'educazione e formazione nel contesto attuale', in V. Orlando (ed.), Con Don Bosco educatori dei giovani del nostro tempo, 145–149.

reasonable source of meaning, a vision of life. Therefore, we can speak of the wisdom of the act of faith: in addition to being possible and legitimate, the experience of a religious faith is also plausible. The religious act is thus the personal, rational and free response to the call to 'be'. We can consider that, when a person motivated in terms of ethical and religious values, the whole person is challenged in the exercise of his or her freedom and responsibility.

Humankind can only adequately satisfy the question of the meaning of existence within these parameters. 'Meaninglessness' means precisely living without a purpose in life. Much of a person's existential strength depends on how they present and resolve the religious question.

3. Now, if the aim of education is to place the person at the centre, ensuring harmony between the various dimensions, mediation (of people, processes, instruments or structures) is the indisputable facilitating element. To mediate is to bring together, to enrich, to help to find points of reference. In this sense, the Salesian educator knows themselves to be a mediator, moving between their experience and the newness of the young person; between the meaning of life that they themselves are building and those who are beginning their journey through it; between the difficulty of accompanying and the ability to allow themselves to be accompanied. The most important aspects of life, those that give it meaning and significance, are not learned, not received and do not appear by chance; rather, they require facilitators who promote research, reflection and decision-making. The Salesian educator does not have cast-iron certainties, they accept and understand the complexity of every young person; they are a humble cartographer who shares with the young people their own handmade maps, which, like a good explorer, they always adapt.

For this Salesian educational intervention to be effective (because it is affective, as we will explain later), it cannot take place in a relationship between two strangers. The essential starting point is the personal encounter with young people and the personal exercise of listening attentively to their demands and aspirations, of valuing the potential for growth that each one of them has within him or herself.

—Evangelising: do we all have same understanding?

Evangelising is the proclamation of the Gospel which the Church carries out in the world through all that she says, does and is. The Church's reflection on evangelisation moves every believer to bring the richness, the depth, the integrity and the many expressions of the message close to him or her. Jesus of Nazareth is the foundation of the Church's vocation and mission in the world: proclaiming the Gospel is the deepest identity of the ecclesial community.

Evangelising is a complex process with multiple components; its understanding takes into account all the aspects and dimensions of Jesus' mission, all his ministry for the sake of the Kingdom. From this point of view, evangelising, in its broadest sense, involves kerygma, human promotion and inculturation:

• the extension of the Kingdom and its values among all people, acting at the service of the proclamation of Jesus Christ and his message; a Kingdom that is already at work in the life of those who welcome it;

• the progressive drawing in of people closer to the ideals and values of the Gospel: the rejection of violence and war; the right to freedom, justice, peace and fraternity; the overcoming of discrimination; the affirmation of the dignity and worth of every person;

• active intervention in areas of the modern world, such as the promotion of women and children, the safeguarding of creation, international relations and the world of social communication; equally, diligent action in the large areas or sectors where humanity suffers: refugees, migrants, new generations, emerging peoples, minorities, lands of oppression, misery and catastrophes.

The dynamics of the total process of evangelisation is defined in a number of aspects: presence, witness, preaching (explicit proclamation), call to personal conversion, formation of the Church, catechesis; and also inculturation, interreligious dialogue, education, preferential option for the poor, the transformation of society. Its complexity and articulation have been authoritatively highlighted by *Evangelii Nuntiandi* (n. 17) and perfectly presented in *Redemptoris Missio* (nn. 41–60).[7]

---

7   The encyclical *Redemptoris missio* (December 7, 1990) takes up the legacy of the Council twenty-five years after its celebration (and fifteen years after the promulgation of Paul VI's *Evangelii nuntiandi*).

Pope Francis' exhortation *Evangelii Gaudium* (*EG*) recapitulates this understanding of evangelisation of the last half century, takes up the magisterium of the Council and previous popes and assumes the main lines of the two documents cited above. The Pope details elements such as the joy of evangelising; the figure of the Church centred on mission;[8] the revolution of tenderness communicated in the Gospel of mercy; the social dimension of the Gospel and of evangelisation; as well as the option for the poor from the heart of God. It also proposes a revision of behaviours and structures so that "the original freshness of the Gospel" (*EG* 19) and its "central nucleus" (*EG* 34) may reach everyone (*EG* 19–49).

This broad vision of evangelisation corroborates the first obligation of the Salesian mission: the holistic development of people, according to the needs of the many different concrete situations. Working in this field, inspired by the love of Christ and under the banner of his Kingdom, is evangelising.

—Strange travelling companions?

The dynamic of the Salesian model shows the mutual relationship between education and evangelisation. The former is enriched by being inspired by the Gospel from the outset; the latter, right from the start, recognises the need to be properly acclimatised to the evolving condition of young people, and by releasing all the educational potential of Christ's message, it leads to human maturity, enlightens, invites and challenges freedom.

From what we have seen so far, we can affirm that the intent of 'educational action' is in itself distinct from the intent of 'evangelising action'; each has its own characteristic purpose, as well as its own unique ways and contents. We must know how to distinguish them, not to separate them, but to unite them harmoniously in practice. Both act on the unity of the person, of the young person; they are two complementary approaches that converge in an attempt to 'engender' the new person. Like Don Bosco, we need a profound and realistic vision of the person, of their human condition, of their origin and spiritual destiny. This anthropological approach leads us to a better understanding of

---

8 The Pope himself calls to move from a "self-referential" Church to a "Church going out", committed to "the peripheries", like a "field hospital", according to his well-known expressions (cf. *EG* 4–49).

how the Salesian educator's activities are marked by an integral humanism and, at the same time, by a transcendent dimension.

Although it is not always easy to 'assemble' the human and faith dimensions, both are shaped to collaborate fully in the singular and integral growth of the person. The two dimensions mutually permeate each other: Christian formation flourishes in a balanced and committed (educated) personality; culture opens the way to faith, looks to its understanding and allows itself to be challenged. The purpose of the of the following sections it to understand the true meaning and fruitfulness of this mutual relationship.

—**Evangelising is measured on the human level.** Education, by helping people to attain a fuller life, is of interest to all those who wholeheartedly desire the good of humanity. Consequently, education is the place where we present the Gospel and where it acquires a typical character. Seen in this way, the education of young people is not an optional manifestation of charity: the Salesian formative interest recognises that God's action passes through the educational mediations of the Church.

1. On the other hand, it is necessary to recognise that faith develops on that intimate level between God and the person, which escapes any attempt at external mediation. Salvific grace itself possesses an immeasurable educative power, not measurable by the human eye. We can affirm that in the relationship between humankind and God, where faith is a gift in the fullest sense, only the primacy of God is possible.

To all of the above, however, we must add that the interventions are aimed at bringing about an encounter that is hardly immediate or direct, because it refers to a mysterious reality. For our part, we want to affirm that the offer of faith and salvation is shown in an ordinary way. Its power and effectiveness are conditioned, for better or for worse, by the human way of transmitting it and by the availability of the person who receives it.

In other words: evangelising is measured on the human level it encounters. It is measured by the anthropological dynamisms that education facilitates, it is measured by educational processes and dynamics where the Gospel of Jesus Christ can resonate, as a condition for it to be accepted in its truth. The Christian message is thus presented in an educational perspective, it is offered in the context of a scheme that favours true and integral growth, takes on and regenerates daily life and gives meaning and fullness to all that is going on around it. The power of faith is never trivialised or manipulated; it is not reduced to a simple educational process.

2. The dynamic proposed here is tailored towards making an existentially meaningful proposal of faith, to make the signs of salvation transparent and in tune with the young person's capacity for acceptance and response. The educational-pastoral model allows itself to be challenged by the experience of young people, recognises the ultimate questions that are in their hearts and, therefore, allows faith and the proclamation of the Gospel to converse fruitfully with them, in a language that is both accessible and didactic, and culturally significant. In this sense, education assumes a positive critical role regarding certain forms of evangelisation which can err on the side of naivety and abstraction.

Education for human and Christian maturity immediately evokes a pedagogical perspective: it activates, sustains, mediates the Gospel mission with educational realism. The priority of God's intervention unfolds by means of mediations and educational signs that tend to enliven the dialogue of salvation, to prepare and sustain the free response and to liberate personal resources.

Since education is a process and is continually called to adapt to the evolution of the person, the proposal of faith must take care of the gradualness of the journey in the form of an itinerary: it is a proposal *in itinere* (ongoing), that is, in continuous reformulation and realisation, in order to relate the expectations of the person and the offer of faith and salvation. We are talking about the interaction between personal experience and Christian experience, between the psychodynamics of personality and the spiritual life.

3. For its part, true Christian humanism is the meeting place of civilisation and culture. Evangelising requires attention to the tangible circumstances of each individual, who demands to be heard and listened to in 'their' situation, in the actual experience of their lives, in order to be helped on the path of personal development, which will never take place on the margins or outside the 'here and now' of society. Recognising the issues of diverse cultures allows faith and the proclamation of the Gospel to converse fruitfully with them.

The educational-pastoral model is convinced that it is the bearer of a message rich in human and spiritual values, which it wants to be faithful to, and, at the same time, to have a mission of service to society. It is proving to be highly relevant today in the most diverse contexts, even outside the frontiers of the 'Catholic world'. It has already proven its validity in environments of various religious traditions, multicultural contexts and secularised areas. Today, however, in the mosaic of extremely culturally and religiously pluralistic societies, it is clear that Christian references cannot always be explicitly stated. They need to be interpreted and adapted to accentuate the humanism of the whole; the basic platform of all education, open to the ethical and religious dimension, should be emphasised. Humanism gives due importance to knowledge and appreciation of the cultures and spiritual values of various civilisations.

The Salesian work, in virtue of its universal vocation and challenged by the presence of different religions and beliefs, is called to use the 'vocabulary of dialogue' with other religious and spiritual traditions. It is not a matter of proclaiming one's own identity, much less of assuming fundamentalist attitudes. What is called for today is to fully know the educational-pastoral model at our disposal, applying it in harmony with modern cultural practices, with their promises and hopes. Religious pluralism is an opportunity for a better understanding of educational and evangelising identity. In this sense, awareness of one's own identity is the irrevocable condition for any fruitful dialogue.

This perspective expresses the need for a profound inculturation of the Preventive System: with those who do not accept God, to make a journey together, based on the human and lay values of the Preventive System; with those who accept God or transcendence, to go further and encourage the acceptance of religious values; finally, with those who share faith in Christ, but not in the Church, to take even greater care in witness and dialogue.

On the other hand, the radical inspiration of the educational process is the Gospel. Whoever operates in the field of education immediately discovers the need to define a type of person in order to determine the direction of his or her educational programme. They realise that they need an anthropological vision with which to measure themself. Consequently, the educator perceives that the evaluative and operative criteria that are inspired by Jesus Christ interpret life in a way that is in keeping with the Gospel. They are the key to a new humanity, they become part of the inner balance of the person's formation. Jesus Christ, the man who is entirely free and entirely for others, saves humanly.

In fact, the most genuine Salesian educational action is rooted in that of Jesus Christ; it not only takes it as a model, but it prolongs it over time. It finds its integral meaning and a reason of major force in his message. Moreover, it finds in the Gospel the guide to orient itself in its own projects, the illumination to mature the seeds of life. The Gospel inspires criteria of judgment, directs fundamental life choices, enlightens the private and public ethical conscience, and regulates interpersonal relationships. It presents itself as an excellent inspiration for the authenticity of love and offers the clearest and most committed horizon of the social dimension of the person. Ultimately, the dignity of the person is elevated in the interaction with the faith of the Gospel. In the words of Pope Benedict XVI:

> Their [Salesians] charism places them in the privileged situation of being able to appreciate the contribution of education in the field of the evangelisation of youth. Without education, in fact, there is no lasting and profound evangelisation, no growth or maturation, no change in mentalities and cultures. Young people harbour a deep desire for a full life, for genuine love, for constructive freedom; but unfortunately, their expectations are often betrayed and come to nothing. It is indispensable to help the young to make the most of their inner resources, such as dynamism and positive aspirations; to put before them proposals that are rich in humanity and Gospel values; to urge them to integrate themselves into society as an active part of it through work and participation and commitment to the common good.[9]

If the Salesian understanding of evangelisation is animated by a concern for wholeness, followed by an educational concern for the growth of the whole person, the proclamation of Jesus Christ does not come afterwards. They are not two phases or stretches of a path: one, educational competence, and the other, the later action of faith. This perspective that we have presented overcomes the essentially methodological problem of how and when to proclaim the

---

9   Benedict XVI, *Letter to the Very Reverend Pascual Chávez Villanueva, SDB on The Occasion of The General Chapter of The Salesians of Don Bosco*, From the Vatican, 1 March 2008.

Gospel and how to combine all the dimensions of the educational-pastoral model in educational environments and programmes.

However, if the ultimate aim of educational mediation is to positively guide the process of configuration to Christ, the perfect man, not all educational models offer this valuable service. We recognise ourselves in an educational praxis that is never an exploitation of faith, that does not render strategies, contents and resources absolute; that manages the educational process in an open way, with an unpredictable, non-manipulative result, because it has to do with the mystery of people's freedom and of God's action in the life of each person and in the life of groups and institutions.

3. Parameters for the Appropriate Development of Salesian Institutions

'Mission, vision and values' are not concepts that point only to strategic issues in an institution. 'Mission' is the indicator of any collective project; it points to the direction to follow to avoid wrong turnings. 'Vision' conveys what we are now compared with what we want to become, which keeps us heading towards the ideal. 'Values' represent shared beliefs and the guidelines to follow in relationships. In our case, they help us understand the goals of the Salesian model.

When we (re)read of the pedagogical-pastoral legacy of Don Bosco, we admire in him a package of vitality and action: first of all, identified throughout his life with the cause of young people, with their individual and social destiny, he promoted strong support for action, a 'corporal' charity concerned with basic needs (food, clothing, housing, work,[10] education); secondly, he was characterised by a pastoral interest, summarised in the expression the "salvation of souls"; finally, he dedicated much energy to the spiritual animation of the religious and educational communities founded by him.

---

10   Cf. S. Tramontin, 'Don Bosco y el mundo del trabajo', in *Don Bosco in History: Proceedings of the First International Congress of Studies on Saint John Bosco, Pontifical Salesian University - Rome, January 16–20, 1989*, Online: https://www.sdb.org/en/Don_Bosco/Biographical_Material/Documents/Don_Bosco_en_la_Historia_UPS_1989 [Accessed 20/06/2022].

To realise the future scenario that he wanted for his project, he tried to involve the widest circle of people from the beginning: catechists, teachers, instructors, technicians, educators, animators, benefactors, religious and civil authorities. He invited many people and groups to a spiritual union and to an educational and evangelising participation. Today, this commitment to the future of the Salesian educational-pastoral model can be expressed in an educational DNA that distinguishes the Salesian institutions: their reason for being (mission), what they want to become and achieve (vision) and the broad framework of values that define them.

3.1. Mission: an essential motive in every institution

With the mission we mainly define the purpose of every institution and its uniqueness or differentiating aspect. The mission is the answer to the question: what is the *raison d'être*, what identifies the Salesian educational-pastoral model in comparison with other educational proposals? In some way, the 'why' of our existence must continue to illuminate what we do today.

We understand that the mission of the Salesians of Don Bosco participates in the evangelising mission of the Church. Through education and evangelisation, they accompany children, adolescents and young people, with particular attention to the most disadvantaged, in the integral growth of all their characteristics as individuals. This offer expresses the willingness to engage in a welcoming and personalised care with an anthropological, pedagogical and spiritual approach ("good Christians and honest citizens"), based on the values of the Gospel and on the educational system of Don Bosco.

The wise and brief formulation referring to the duty to train citizens to build the city and be people of faith, must be understood with all the signs that characterise today's society. Between the statements "good Christians" and "honest citizens",[11] there is an inescapable relationship of reciprocity. This is a slogan that has not lost its validity and they both synthesise the main purposes that must be known, understood and shared by all those who constitute a

---

11   E. Ceria and D. Borgatello, *Biographical Memoirs of St John Bosco.* (New Rochelle, NY: Salesiana Publishers, 1983) [*BM*], vol. XIII, 480. (original: *Memorie biografiche di Don Bosco,* 19 vols. Turin: San Benigno Canavese, I-IX [1898–1917], by G. B. Lemoyne; X [1939], by A. Amadei; XI- XIX [1930–1939], by E. Ceria).

Salesian presence and who form the educational-pastoral community (religious, young people, educators, parents, etc.), as we will see later.

Four convictions are paramount in this mission:

• an education centred on Jesus, who is presented as a model and from whom love and respect for each young person is promoted through his or her dignity as a person;

• a preferential option for the working classes and the most needy young people, the centre and purpose of the Salesian educational-pastoral approach. They must be and are, in fact, active subjects, protagonists of evangelisation and architects of social renewal;

• a deep commitment to the transformation of the person and of society;

• an integral and integrating formative proposal in the development of people's capacities, paying attention to the transcendent, cognitive, cultural, ethical, aesthetic, emotional and corporal dimensions as well as to solidarity.

3.2. Vision: the main goal in people's hearts

The vision defines the goals to be achieved. Being a 'visual image' of what an institution would like to be, these goals have an inspirational and motivating character, and, in the case of the Salesian methodology, they respond to the questions: where do we want to be in the future and where are we going? What are the immediate challenges? What traces do we want to leave in society and in young people for their growth and development? What do we want to obtain for new generations from Salesian education?

We consider that the Salesians of Don Bosco want to be recognised for:

• offering children and young people pathways of development for the formation of integral, caring and committed people, enabling their holistic development and preparing them to achieve their autonomy and personal success in society;

• fostering relationships of trust between all members of the educational-pastoral community, in order to create a family atmosphere or environment, respecting differences of sex, race, culture and religion;

38

- trusting in the possibilities of personal growth of each one, taking care of positive stimulating environments that favour personal encounter, encounter with others, with society and with God;

- educating in a constant dialogue with faith and culture, achieving maximum personal freedom, responsibility and a critical vision of reality.

As can be seen, it is a 'choral' vision that encompasses the experience of young people, the dreams of their educators and the concerns of families. As Peter M Senge, an American economist, educationalist and writer rightly puts it: "A shared vision is not an idea. It is a force in people's hearts, a force of awesome power. It may be inspired by an idea, but if it is compelling enough to win the support of more than one person, it is no longer just a dream. It is palpable. People begin to see it as if it exists. Few human forces are as powerful as a shared vision."[12]

3.3. Values: models that identify and guide the educational task

To conclude this chapter, we will point out the institutional values, the traits on which the culture of the mission is based and which make it possible to create guidelines for behaviour, style and organisation. In this case, they are the personal traits of every Salesian presence. Some arise from our concepts of the human person, their social condition and transcendence. Obviously, behind each and every one of them is the Christian concept of the human being, because every educational practice is preceded by a worldview or a way of understanding the person. Others, on the other hand, come from the incessant transformations in culture and in the world. They are all values in accordance with the historical moment of contemporary society.

The values we propose are the answer to how we are and what we believe in (mission), they are identified with aspirations, the way we act and how we view life (vision).

Although we will go through most of these fundamental and constant elements of the Salesian educational-pastoral model in these pages, here is a summary of these values:

---

12   P.M. Senge, *The Fifth Discipline. How to boost learning in the intelligent organisation*, (Buenos Aires: Granica, 2005), 260–261.

Respect for every life and special care for the weakest.
Unconditional welcome and affectionate presence.
Responsible leadership and civil commitment.
Co-responsibility and teaching of everyday duties.
Personal growth and spirituality.
Educational-pastoral creativity and diversity of offerings.

These values must have a presence, they are the backbone of the life of the centres, and they are closely related to the great pillars of Don Bosco's educational and pastoral experience.

Chapter Two

The Outlook and the Path Followed by the Educational Work of Don Bosco

1. Google Maps for the 'Oratory City'

In this chapter we will explore the most significant milestones in the history of Don Bosco the educator, his origins in informal, school and vocational education. In this way we will be in a better position to decipher and understand the themes, the principles and the devices that underlie the inspirational founding framework of the Salesian educational-pastoral model: the Preventive System.[1]

---

1   Excellent studies from the point of view of historical methodology that reconstruct the context, work and thought of Don Bosco are those of P. Stella, *Don Bosco nella storia della religiosità cattolica*, (Zürich-Rome: LAS), the three volumes ▷

It is not an easy task to examine a single and isolated dimension of Don Bosco in this educational work, given that he presents himself as a very diverse character: a man of his time, priest, educator, worker, writer, social worker and saint.[2]

1. The fundamental strands of Don Bosco's educational experience are typically expressed in the character of the institutions where he and his collaborators worked: "Deeds, works, are his being and his message."[3] They can only be understood in conjunction with various factors:

• first of all, his biography, which makes his educational action 'unique', and in some ways prophetic;[4]

• secondly, his temperament, typical of a well-balanced person: soft and strong, human and spiritual, grounded in his homeland and driven by his dreams;

• thirdly, his personality as a leader: charismatic, entrepreneurial, innovative, communicative, an extraordinary organiser, tenacious in pursuing his objectives and flexible in dealing with practical situations;

• finally, his activity on behalf of young people, especially those suffering from poverty, abandonment, homelessness and destitution.

---

of which appeared in 1968, 1969 and 1988, and the thirty-five chapters of P. Braido's monumental work, *Don Bosco The Young People's Priest In The Century of Freedoms*, 2 vols. (Rome: LAS, 2009) (Italian original: *Don Bosco, prete dei giovani nel secolo delle libertà*, (Rome, LAS, 2003)).

2   In the preface to the first volume of Braido, *Don Bosco The Young People's Priest In The Century of Freedoms*, the author defines Don Bosco as "free and faithful; traditional and progressive, communicative and reserved; bold and thoughtful" and "realist and dreamer".

3   Ibid., I, 17.

4   For an understanding of Don Bosco, his place and his time, we refer to Appendix 1 of our study. As an adolescent, he studied and lived for ten years in the town of Chieri (population about 9,000), a town populated by convents, weavers and students; he carried out his activities in an urban environment, in a city of Turin which was increasingly taking on the characteristics of an industrial and financial city, and which, through the newly emerging middle class, was preparing to become the driving force of national unity. The transition from an agricultural and artisanal society to one with an industrial structure was bringing about its demographic and social transformation.

In this chapter we will try to document and briefly outline the historical and spiritual journey[5] that emerges from the priest-educator, and, with it, the educational approach and the environment created by that gifted personality.

Indeed, to understand this priest of exceptional pastoral intelligence, it is necessary to retrace his personal and community educational journey from a very young age. He acquired a long-range vision of faith that sought to penetrate and grasp the depths of events, a sustained gaze, pierced and enveloped by the mystery of God. He is an attentive observer of his world and a watchful witness to the new times, conditioning factors, motivations, influences and interactions; he also lived in an era when Catholic teaching was swinging between traditionalism and innovation.

2. In fact, it is essential to consider this turbulent environment in which his work developed, which in part inspired and conditioned it.[6]

Industrial development, urban growth and patriotic aspirations towards national unity had made Turin a centre of immigration for the Piedmontese provinces and for Italy as a whole. It was also the capital of a large kingdom, perhaps the largest in territorial terms in the Italian context, and therefore in a position to apply pressure on the most vulnerable groups.

---

5   To delve deeper into the life and work of Don Bosco, we suggest reading the seven volumes of A.J. Lenti, *Don Bosco: History and Spirit*, edited by Aldo Giraudo, (Rome: LAS, 2007). The first three volumes survey the life and times of John Melchior Bosco up to 1864, with particular attention to nineteenth-century political, social and religious history, discussing Don Bosco's own education, his spiritual and theological formation leading to his priestly ordination (1841). The next four volumes describe Don Bosco's life and work in the period following the unification of Italy, a period marked by epochal changes in Italian society. It discusses the institutional developments and organisation of the Salesian Society through the stages of the approval of the institute and of the constitutions by the Holy See. It describes Don Bosco's further ministerial choices, especially in the field of education, and his further founding work. It surveys the expansion of the Salesian work to parts of Italy and to European and South American countries. At the same time, it examines the development of permanent structures to guarantee the continuance of the Salesian work, and discusses some of the founder's insights and ideas, especially as they emerge from the reflective writings of his maturity.

6   See a well elaborated synthesis of the historical context in the Salesian Historical Institute, *Salesian Sources I. Don Bosco and His Work*, (Rome: LAS, 2014).

At the political level, the separation between Church and State was concluded. The Church lost, with the abolition of Religious Orders and the seizure of its goods, its traditional places of assembly and instruction. The labour question and the social mentality put the Church in a new situation that demanded an effort to connect with the most significant groups in society: young people, workers, immigrants and intellectuals. Popular culture, therefore, traditionally informed by a Christian spirit, suffered the onslaught of political and economic changes, the insecurity resulting from the law of freedom of belief and a process of collective amnesia towards religious truths.

Parish structures were inappropriate for this new social order. Dependent young people, apprentices and students were deprived of moral and religious assistance. The problem of 'poor and abandoned youth' became urgent in Turin. In short, Don Bosco had to adapt himself to the complicated historical, political, cultural and ecclesial context of the nineteenth century.

3. The title of this section could also be the 'educational workshop' of Valdocco, as Fr Braido happily called this experience. Don Bosco put together an articulated response, a series of multiple functional initiatives with the intention of meeting the needs of the working class and youth: It began with the Oratory, an open environment for meeting and living together, for relaxation and instruction, designed to tackle the situation of educational and religious abandonment in which young people find themselves; it continued with the school-workshop-residence, a complex institution that offered a comprehensive education adapted to the new needs of training for work. In addition to this, there are the educational and religious publications with which the people of the town could be reached through the most modern means and in an easy style, always with the pastoral focus of reminding them of the truths of the faith and promoting their culture.

As can be seen, this way of subdividing the world of education into various and diverse works responds to different needs (assistance, school, professional, catechetical, formative), with similar educational content and methods. What is certain is that Don Bosco tried to reach the greatest number of people and to respond to the entirety of their educational and evangelising concerns. One cannot ignore, therefore, the different character that each environment assumes; each institution has, in fact, its own originality and its specific recipients. That is why he did not give priority to any of these environments but rather sought to satisfy the young people's demands for security, friendship and work, including other equally important ones, such as spirituality, play and happiness.[7]

Undoubtedly, this 'Oratory' built in the district of Valdocco created a particular style of educating which made it possible to incarnate its educational spirit. For this reason, the personnel sent to establish and direct distant works had to be formed in this same place. Don Bosco had made a school and created traditions with those young collaborators, but at the same time he was enriched by the experiences of his disciples, immersed like him in the daily incidents of an educational environment of enormous mobility and full of surprises.[8]

2. Roots of Salesian Identity: A Photofit

It is true that the theological and educational horizon of Don Bosco is different from today's; his formative curriculum had endowed him with experience and knowledge that allowed him to respond to the needs of his time. From examining these roots, we can visualise some original intentions and intuitions that have survived the passage of time and are still highly relevant today.

The saintly educator not only pursued the establishment of his oratorian vision, but also its more organic, diversified and meaningful outreach. Braido himself identified two distinct elements in his action: on the one hand, the "priest of the young in the Church of Turin"; on the other, the founder "for the youth of the world."[9]

1. The main objective of these pages is to learn about the *raison d'être* of his works and their popular character. It is therefore striking to recall that he has always been able to respond to challenges with a determination to be among young people and to make original ideas to them: In his childhood, he gathered his friends in the meadows near his home; in the hayloft of his first

---

7   Cf. B. Delgado, 'Don Bosco, pedagogue of joy', in *Don Bosco in history*.

8   Cf. Braido, *Don Bosco The Young People's Priest In The Century of Freedoms*,II, 260–261.

9   Ibid.

place of work on the Moglia farm; as a seminarian he combined catechism with games and private lessons; as a student at Chieri he joined the Society of Joy, founded to help his fellow students with their studies and pious practices; at the *Convitto Ecclesiastico*, he accompanied his teacher and director Joseph Cafasso on a visit to the prisons of Turin, a place where Don Bosco himself said he was "disconcerted". From all these experiences, the Oratory was finally born.

The work of Don Bosco came into being with few institutional characteristics on December 8, 1841. It began significantly with a simple catechetical lesson "in the room next to the church of St Francis of Assisi",[10] which was immediately completed with the charity of bread, the alms of clothing, physical sustenance and the means to provide it honestly. Charity already existed and there were social initiatives in the Church of Turin, but for Don Bosco there was another idea of charity. To put it in a nutshell: offering bread together with education.

Charity manifests itself as the "perfection of love"[11] which he makes the main proposal of his whole spirituality.

It is a programme of life that expresses itself in daily gestures; it is a pedagogical principle that activates its best resources to care for the children.

2. Don Bosco communicated in words and in writing his plans and proposed various possibilities for the application of his preventive educational system. In fact, the guidelines and the stories he left us, the experience he passed on to us, are added to the numerous institutions founded, animated or directed by him. Reference to these institutions is the cornerstone for understanding the evolution and the coordinated construction of the "system"; they can in fact be classified into two broad categories: more open ones, such as youth clubs, festive and daily oratories, evening and Sunday schools, the mass press; and other more structured institutions, such as orphanages, boarding schools for students and tradesmen, vocational schools, colleges and seminaries.

In the former, total spontaneity of freedom to come and go, with little burden of disciplinary and organisational norms; it also aims at contact with the

---

10   E. Ceria, *Annali della Società Salesiana dalle origini alla morte di S. Giovanni Bosco (1841-1888)*, I. (Turin: SEI, 1941) 103.

11   St Francis de Sales, *Treatise on the Love of God* II, Book X, Chapter 1.

family and with the young person's outside world. There is a constant dialogue between what has been learnt and everyday life, and the troublesome problem of economic dealings (monthly payments or pensions) lost its relevance.

In the latter, from 1862 onwards, the collegial regime made teaching and learning more systematic, and this allowed the original values of the Preventive System to be established, although not without some adjustments. As can be expected, schools and boarding schools demanded specific qualities, training and educational wisdom from their educators.

All of them, except for the missions, which began in January 1880, are globally incorporated in the text of the Constitutions, which were officially approved in April 1874.[12]

> The first act of charity will be to gather together poor and abandoned young people in order to instruct them in the Catholic religion, especially on feast days. ...There are also those who live abandoned in such a way that any care is useless to them if they are not taken in; therefore, as far as possible, boarding schools will be opened where, with the means that Divine Providence will place in our hands, they will be provided with lodging, food and clothing, and, at the same time, they will be instructed in the truths of the faith; moreover, they will be initiated in an art or trade, as is done at present in the house attached to the Oratory of St Francis de Sales in this city.[13]

The Oratory was the cradle where all his early intuitions were born. It was the 'little kingdom of Valdocco', increasingly populated by adolescents, to which Don Bosco dedicated his daily care and, at the same time, where he directly tested his educational ideas.[14] The subsequent development of these are complementary institutions: orphanages and colleges were not differentiated from the pedagogical point of view, since the moral and religious education of the boys was considered in the same way.

---

12   Some structures were not created by Don Bosco from the beginning, but are typical of the Restoration era, many of them with roots in the distant era of the Catholic Reformation, but which receive from his system a new philosophy.

13   G. Bosco, *Costituzioni della Società di S. Francesco di Sales [1858]–1875.* (Rome: LAS, 1982), 75 (arts. III y IV).

14   Cf. Braido, *Don Bosco The Young People's Priest In The Century of Freedoms.* I, 401.

2.1. Two sides of the same coin: students and artisans

Valdocco was, par excellence, the archetype and the centre of animation of a new type of work that was to become the setting for the educational-pastoral approach; together with the schools and the arts and crafts workshops, preferably organised within the collegial and oratory environment, the festive or daily Oratory was added as an integral part.

1. The first welfare-educational structure to appear, in 1846, was the daily or festive Oratory. The permanent establishment of the Oratory was located in Valdocco, the 'Sunday' home of underprivileged young people: without a family or abandoned by them, resident workers or immigrants without any fixed abode, ex-prisoners, cleaners, apprentice bricklayers and painters looking for work, students, and so on.[15]

This is the place where the pedagogical experience of Don Bosco is born and matures: it is the first work both chronologically and in terms of educational and apostolic importance. The Oratory was forged from the immediate needs of these young people and was instantly filled with formative elements: catechesis, religious practice, recreational and cultural activities, gymnastics, excursions.[16] The Oratory was forged in the Piedmontese culture with the presence, first of all, of Margaret, the mother of Don Bosco and mother of all those boys: her familiar dialect gave a popular tone to the friendly and homely atmosphere. Secondly, devotions, theatre[17] and song[18] created, together with music, a vibrant school, full of popular expressions, fables and myths.

---

15   In 1847 and 1849 he established two more Oratories under the patronage of St Aloysius Gonzaga and the Guardian Angel, respectively.

16   U. M. Gallego Gago, *El tiempo libre en el sistema educativo de Don Bosco*, (Madrid: Universidad Complutense, 1987).

17   Cf. M. Bongioanni, *Don Bosco y el teatro*, (Madrid: CCS, 1991); S. Pivato, 'Don Bosco y el teatro popular', in *Don Bosco in History*; T. Lewicki, 'Il volto e la missione del teatro educativo salesiano', in A. Giraudo, G. Loparco, J. M. Prellezo, G. Rossi (eds.), *Sviluppo del carisma di Don Bosco fino alla metà del secolo XX. Comunicazioni*, (Rome: LAS, 2016), 259–277.

18   Cf. M. Rigoldi, *Don Bosco y la música*, (Madrid: CCS, 1991); G. Sforza, 'Don Bosco y la música', in *Don Bosco in History*; J. Gregur, 'La musica, "anima" del carisma salesiano', in Giraudo et al., *Sviluppo del carisma di Don Bosco fino alla metà del secolo*, 102–121.

Together with the Oratory, we should mention various types of popular schools that would acquire their own importance in Don Bosco's work as a whole: singing and music schools, literacy and general education schools, which gave life to the evening and Sunday schools. In time, years later, the morning day schools were opened (1857).

2. However, the institution which, together with the Oratory, was to be the focus of Don Bosco's best energies was undoubtedly the orphanage (1847), later converted into a boarding school for students and artisans, orphans and boys of humble origin who went to work or to school in the city. For some years it was also called 'the annex house' because it was next to the Oratory of the day pupils.

In those first six or seven years of the orphanage, the lack of space did not allow for more than fifteen or so residents;[19] For this reason Don Bosco endeavoured during this period to give it stability and greater possibilities of acceptance in its dual purpose of residence and festive oratory.[20]

In fact, between 1859 and 1867, the number of boarders in the house rose from 300 to 800, according to the data we have from Don Bosco himself.

3. Consequently, there was a growing need to give a pedagogical form to the norms of ordinary life, to codify and organise them, and so a series of regulations was gradually drawn up; thus the 'Regulations for the houses of the Society of St Francis de Sales' (1877) translates the pedagogical inspirations into rules of behaviour, coexistence and organisation. However, the norm here adopts the tone and language of "a father who speaks to his children" and of "a friend who advises the young", so that what is to be done may be carried out successfully, joyfully and in collaboration.

It is important to clarify that the structure of the boarding school was not only a shelter for 'abandoned' boys, but also lodging for high school students between 1855 and 1859, and for some seminarians and orphaned apprentices

---

19   Cf. Braido, *Don Bosco The Young People's Priest In The Century of Freedoms*.

20   In 1850 he bought a piece of land that belonged to the seminary; the following year he bought the Pinardi house with the little roof, with the threshing floor, the garden and part of the orchard, for 28,000 lire.

(boys aged 12–18 who worked in the city all day and could not afford the costs of their lodging and maintenance). This is how Don Bosco describes it:

> While we worked to set up ways of supplying instructions in religion and literacy, another crying need became evident; it was urgent to make some provision for it. Many youngsters from Turin and migrants [were] quite willing to try to live hard-working and moral lives; but when they were encouraged to begin, they used to answer that they had no bread, no clothing, and no shelter where they could stay at least for a while. ... Convinced that for many children every effort would prove useless unless they were offered shelter, I set about renting more and more rooms, even though the cost was exorbitant.[21]

4. From 1853 onwards, Don Bosco set up a modest shoemaking workshop for young apprentices, to be followed by many others. From that time on, together with the many who attended humanities courses, the trades and crafts section would occupy an increasingly important place in the Oratory of St Francis de Sales. From this year until 1862, he gradually organised workshops in the educational complex of Valdocco. The establishment of this section for young workers was a response to the needs of the Piedmontese working class and for academic educational institutions. Strategically, Don Bosco not only created schemes for learning these trades, but also guaranteed favourable conditions for living together with the students. In this way, he gave equal consideration to the dignity of both forms of work.

5. With the provision of secondary education in the Valdocco boarding school, Don Bosco established his first boarding school officially recognised by the state. Similar demands would later (1871–1872) lead to the organisation of elementary day schools Don Bosco wrote to the Mayor of Turin:

> An overflowing number asking for help because of family neglect or because they were badly dressed or because of laziness, were wandering around all over the place. It is necessary to give free instruction to all of them; to not a few of them, even the school supplies, books, paper, pens, etc., and to

---

21 G. Bosco, *Memoirs of the Oratory of Saint Francis de Sales 1815 to 1855*, Translated by Daniel Lyons, SDB. With notes and commentary by Eugene Ceria, SDB, Lawrence Castelvecchi, SDB and Michael Mendl, SDB, (New Rochelle, NY: Salesiana Publishers, 1989), [*MO*], 205 & 206.

others, even bread and clothing. This is done only at the expense of a private individual and cannot last very long without special help.[22]

In short, this work, the original creation of which was Valdocco, quickly became a complex educational campus, with an Oratory for externs, a boarding school with two numerous sections for students and trades people, a seminary,[23] workshops and its own schools. From 1865 to 1884,[24] Valdocco was the Motherhouse of Salesian youth work and of the new religious Congregation; a complete centre of material and spiritual help, of religious and moral assistance, of instruction and recreation; in other words, a place of fundamental youth formation:

> Experience has persuaded us that this is the only way to help civil society: to take care of poor children ... All those who would perhaps go on to populate the prisons and who would be a perpetual social scourge become good Christians and good citizens, the glory of the towns where they live and the honour of the family to which they belong, honestly earning the bread of life with their sweat and their work.[25]

---

22   Letter of August 26, 1872: *Epistolario* II, 224–225.

23   From 1860 to 1864, the house of Don Bosco also welcomed seminarians from the dioceses of Piedmont who, for various reasons, did not have their own seminary at that time.

24   This period is very well described in the minutes of the documents in Valdocco: '*Conferenze capitolari*' (1866–1877), the meetings of the '*Capitolo della Casa*' and the '*Conferenze mensili*'. At these meetings of the councils of animation and government in Valdocco, problems concerning community life were discussed: discipline, the moral improvement of the trades people, the presence of the educators at recreation (Salesian assistance for all), questions concerning study and work, the running of the day and evening classes, meals and the cleanliness of the premises. The most varied activities were prepared, such as religious practices, literary evenings, theatre, games, singing and music. Tasks and responsibilities for the smooth running of the festivities were distributed, the results of the festivities were discussed, and problems to be corrected in the future were pointed out. It was a practical school for experienced educators and for those initiated in the art of education, trained in the hard work of the daily field (cf. Braido, *Don Bosco The Young People's Priest In The Century of Freedoms*, II, 261).

25   Letter of September 30, 1877, to Dr Carranza, from Buenos Aires: *Epistolario* III, 221.

From Turin, the institutions spread rapidly like a chain throughout Italy and beyond, in Europe and beyond. Don Bosco the Founder extended the geographical horizon of his vocation.[26]

2.2. The first school and the metamorphosis of the original spirit

The primitive Oratory without walls or doors had undergone a conversion into a solid school institution. The "schooling", as Fr Braido put it, was the desirable and opportune response at that time to facilitate the young people's civil and cultural placement required by the new historical situation.[27]

1. We will dwell briefly on this point, with the intention of making a more precise reflective analysis of what the opening of the schools meant for Don Bosco. Between 1857 and 1858 all the secondary schools (Grammar schools) were established in Valdocco. Don Bosco's concern and skill in opening and improving his popular schools and in choosing suitable teaching staff or training clerics to run them properly is evident. The schools and colleges demanded much effort and toil from Don Bosco due to the requirements of the liberal legislation of the time, and from which context the educational policies were derived, such as the secularisation of teaching and the progressive state monopoly of state education.

Don Bosco never failed to ensure that the Oratory followed the programmes and discipline stipulated by the legal standards. When providing a list of his teaching staff, he would note their qualifications or the commendations on

---

26   G. Chiosso's contribution is very enlightening: 'Educazione e pedagogia salesiana nel primo novecento, dal punto di vista dell'Italia', in A. Giraudo, G. Loparco, J. M. Prellezo, G. Rossi (eds.), *Sviluppo del carisma di Don Bosco fino alla metà del secolo XX. Relazioni*, (Rome: LAS, 2016), 155–186. The sections dedicated to the question of youth in Don Bosco's time and immediately after, the centrality of the festive Oratory, the first pedagogical interests of the Salesians in the 1920s and 1930s and the scenarios introduced by the encyclical *Divini illius Magistri* are particularly valuable.

27   About the crisis of "schooling" suffered by the Oratory of Valdocco we refer to the study of J.M. Prellezo, *Valdocco in the nineteenth century between real and ideal* (1866–1889). *Documents and testimonials*, (Rome: LAS, 1992).

the ability and prestige of his teachers, and, in the case of those who were still in training, he would ask for provisional approval.

In his petition to the government for the authorisation of his schools at the boarding school of Valdocco, dated December 4, 1862, the saint emphasises the Christian and popular nature of his institution:

> Wishing to promote secondary education among the less well-to-do working class, I have started baccalaureate courses for the poor boys residing in this house in order to provide them with study and training in a subject of their choice, so that they may be able to earn an honest living tomorrow... I note, in passing, that the purpose of this House of Studies is to serve as a minor seminary for those young men who..., possessing talent and virtue, they are, however, deprived of the necessary financial means or are unable to finance their studies completely.[28]

Don Bosco began to organise his own schools in the Oratory as an alternative Catholic education to the secularist movement of the State and to the progressive anti-Catholic discontent against any form of Catholic education. Like the Turinese saint, many founders of educational works and religious families sought to maintain a preventive (not repressive) school strongly rooted in the tradition of the Church.

Other factors that led him to send his boys to school were related to the progressive demographic growth of the cities[29] (the result of the serious situation in the countryside) and the abandonment/danger of adolescents in the street.

It is worth remembering here that Don Bosco emphasised and ratified the popular direction of his schools; he was also aware that, without private and even official charity, his schools would not have been able to maintain their original character and respond to the situations of a poor and middle-class population. However, in 1872, he was forced by Archbishop Lorenzo Gastaldi to accept the college for nobles in Valsalice.

---

28   *BM*, VII, 282.

29   Of the total number of young men admitted to Valdocco between 1847 and 1869, only 9.3% were Turinese.

2. This orientation not only marked a change of direction in the history of Don Bosco's educational institutions, but also the birth of a "new" Preventive System, and at the same time a "new" school: a "new" pedagogy, called to take on a family spirit (the school is the 'house'). In that small primitive oratorian world, the hours were divided between the playground, the chapel, the workshop, the school and the orphanage. But with the phenomenon of 'collegialisation', with disciplinary structures and with different economic costs, there was a danger of conditioning and limiting the vitality of the original spirit: the spontaneity of relationships, typical of the oratorian system; the direct contact with the family and social environments that it facilitated; and, above all, the access of the most disadvantaged young people. In other words, the collegiate institution made him rethink the Preventive System.[30]

In the midst of these observations a question arises: *Was Don Bosco free of worries?* We can answer in the negative. He had every reason to be concerned: in the Oratory at the end of the nineteenth century, which was a continuation of the first longed-for Oratory, there were organisational problems and difficulties that tarnished the original values. Don Bosco was aware that the fundamental spirit was in danger of being replaced by an institutional regime that would lead to the loss or blurring of spontaneity in relationships.

At Valdocco, it became necessary to correct in time any deviations or abuses that had been introduced, to find remedies, to provide practical solutions, to monitor results and to determine adjustments. In 1884 Don Bosco wrote a letter which is considered to be a firm statement of the fundamental principles of his educational method. It reveals the best of his formative skills. Here is an excerpt from the document:

> The reason for the present change in the Oratory is that many of the boys no longer have confidence in their superiors. There was a time when all hearts were wide open to their superiors, when the boys loved them and gave them prompt obedience. But now the superiors are thought of precisely as superiors and no longer as fathers, brothers and friends; they are feared and little loved. And so if you want everyone to be of one heart and soul again for the love of Jesus you must break down this fatal barrier of mistrust, and

30   Cf. Braido, *Don Bosco The Young People's Priest In The Century of Freedoms,* I, 310; Stella, *Don Bosco nella storia della religiosità cattolica,* I, 121–123.

replace it with a happy spirit of confidence. ... When this love languishes, things no longer go well. Why do people want to replace love with cold rules? Do you know what this poor old man who has spent his whole life for his dear boys wants from you? Nothing else than, due allowances being made, we should go back to the happy days of the Oratory of old: the days of affection and Christian confidence between boys and superiors; the days when we accepted and put up with difficulties for the love of Jesus Christ; the days when hearts were open with a simple candour; days of love and real joy for everyone. I want the consolation and hope that you will promise to do everything I desire for the good of your souls.[31]

A first reading of this text already allows us to appreciate that these phrases, born of the troubled soul of Don Bosco, sadly foretold institutional changes.[32] It is not only about what was lived from the 1870s onwards in Valdocco, but also the risk that any Salesian educational structure runs today, if it undermines or in fact supersedes interpersonal relationships, impedes or eliminates them, and therefore endangers educational love, the key and synthesis of all Salesian pedagogy.

---

31   *Letter from Rome to the Salesian community of the Oratory of Valdocco*, May 10, 1884. A critical edition by P. Braido, translated by P. Laws with modifications by G. Williams can be found online: https://donboscosalesianportal. org/wp-content/uploads/Letter-from-Rome.pdf [Accessed 22/06/2022].

32   This text entitled 'Letter from Rome', is set in the last years of Don Bosco's life, May 10, 1884. It is a true source of pedagogical knowledge, a "pedagogical poem", as it is called by the scholar and connoisseur of Bosco's work, Pietro Braido. Although they are two letters written by his secretary, Fr G. B. Lemoyne, they were certainly inspired by Don Bosco; he himself signs in his own handwriting the edition addressed to the boys. His concern was to ensure and protect the genuine survival of his educational style, "unity in leadership". To this end he insists on some key points and expresses a clear and simple educational inventory. The open encounter with the boys had become an imposed attendance; the spontaneous huddle in the playground, rigid rows. The whole system seemed to be rebuilt on another basis: the normative precept. This was a serious contamination and weakening of his original educational vision. In the letter, Don Bosco expresses this uneasiness. In the same vein he wrote three letters to the Salesians in America in 1885.

2.3. The first workshops of the Oratory and the trades section (1841–1843)

The particular motivations behind the shift from workshops to vocational training are historical (changes in the world of work and industrialisation), pastoral (work as an educational tool to bring out the full potential of the individual person) and cultural (vocational schools could not remain narrowly reduced to crafts sector).[33]

1. The first thing to say is that from the beginning of his oratorian activity in 1841, Don Bosco was in contact with young 'apprentices' employed in urban workshops. He accompanied them so that they could gradually manage to start their own independent activity, thus endorsing the practice already established by the work of the 'Mendicity Society' (*Obra de la Mendicidad Instruida*).[34]

This limited group of young people who worked in the city was assisted in order to guarantee them a fair contract of employment. One of these contracts is dated February 8, 1852; it is the "agreement" between the master carpenter Giuseppe Bertolino and the young Giuseppe Odasso, a native of Mondovì, "with the intervention of the reverend priest John Bosco, and with the assistance and authorisation of the father of this boy". Bertolino receives Odasso "as an apprentice in the art of carpentry" and undertakes to "teach him this art for two years".[35]

During the years 1847 and 1852, Don Bosco signed this type of contract to help legally organise the work of the young apprentices, avoiding possible exploitation by the employers and favouring fair remuneration. With the practical intuition that was characteristic of Don Bosco, he defended the good of the young apprentice above the economic and commercial interest of the

---

33   Cf. J. M. Prellezo, *Las escuelas profesionales salesianas. Momentos de su historia*, (Madrid: CCS, 2012).

34   It was founded in 1743 on the initiative of citizens concerned about the pitiful situation of the poor and beggars who swarmed the streets of Turin. Its work was based on catechesis, the rudiments of education and attention to their most urgent needs.

35   *Archivio della Società Salesiana* (based in Rome), S. 0596. A copy of the contract of the young Giuseppe Bordone can also be consulted in the same archive.

workshop (contracts, costs and profits).[36] As can be seen, his great interest was to train these young people progressively and fairly, most of whom were migrants from the rural world.

2. Don Bosco separated the sections for craftsmen and students, and proceeded to give a new direction to his early craft workshops (1853–1869), later transformed into 'vocational schools' (1895–1950). In fact, he gradually established further workshops: tailors and shoemakers (1853), bookbinders (1854), carpenters (1856), typographers (1861) and blacksmiths (1862). In addition to the already prominent religious and moral objectives, social, technical and vocational aspects became increasingly important in this brilliant idea, thus creating a successful formula for apprenticeship.

The model used by Don Bosco for working in his workshops was of a pre-industrial type: bosses, workers and apprentices were governed by the following criteria: the apprentice is a worker and a pupil who needs to work and learn to work in order to live; he is at the centre of the teaching and education of the school-workshop; therefore, his well-being is above economic and commercial interests. It is the responsibility of the workshop leader and the workshop master to have a series of attitudes: to teach with the best learning strategies; to keep the apprentice busy and to make sure that the work is suitable to the age and condition of the young person; to give him the right advice for his moral and civic conduct; to treat him well, inspired by charity, rationality, respect, encouragement and help.

At the same time, the young man is responsible for respect, obedience and compliance towards the workshop leader and the masters; the fulfilment of his duty as an apprentice; to answer for any damage or material damage that he may cause through carelessness or bad will.[37]

---

36   This desire to be in the world of the workers and artisans led him to establish the Valdocco Mutual Aid Society (1849), for which he drew up a small set of regulations the following year. Article 1 of these regulations states that the mission of this entity is "to help those comrades who fall ill or who are in need because they have lost their jobs voluntarily". Later, the relations of the Society and the Association with the Conference of St Vincent de Paul were strengthened.

37   From the *Archivio della Società Salesiana* (based in Rome), S. 0596, in L. Panafilo, *Dalla scuola di arte mestieri di Don Bosco all attività di formazione professionale (1860-1915)*, (Milan: CNOS-LES, 1976), 99–101.

The methodology of the vocational schools was becoming clearer and clearer in Don Bosco's mind. With his characteristic insight, he observed, on the one hand, how the social question was becoming irreversibly more acute; on the other hand, the process of craft education was difficult because of the type of boys who were being offered instruction and training for the world of work. However, Don Bosco tried to reduce the difficulties as much as possible: his resolute aim was to form "good Christians and honest citizens". This meant rejecting the discriminatory criteria of the State technical school. For this reason, he was not content to simply support and promote a shop assistant, but that he should be able to have a small personal business, similar to the one in which he had learned his trade at the Oratory.

This reality placed great responsibility on Don Bosco, the craftsman and the professional, not only in the practical aspects of the trade, but also in the intellectual aspects, so that he could respond to the diverse circumstances that arose in the real world. For this reason, Don Bosco gradually wanted to provide the 'artisan' pupils with a cultural formation suited to their condition. In this way, academic education went hand in hand with training for work; in fact, from 1870 onwards, it was customary to bring teachers together to help them with pedagogical criteria and didactic resources in the management of both workshops and academic studies.

At the Oratory, the workshops were consolidated as true centres of professional training, and at the same time they acquired the characteristics of production companies. A clear example of this joint development was the printing service. The owner, the entrepreneur and the formator of the Valdocco workshops was Don Bosco. For him, it was clear that the primary source of income was charity; nevertheless, the workers would have to make some profit that would contribute to the financing and be an incentive for the teachers, the workers and, above all, for the apprentices themselves. This was a profit-making enterprise. From his experience, pedagogical wisdom and priestly zeal, Don Bosco was careful to reaffirm the educational character of his works.

The school-workshop-business model was a challenge for Don Bosco. He had to manage, with his characteristic skill, the administration and control not only of the economics, but also of the quality of the products so that they could compete on the market. Following the example of the typography workshop, by becoming a typographer and publisher, he ensured that the publications of a religious, pedagogical and educational nature responded with quality in content and form.

In 1883, as a result of a new decision discussed at the third General Chapter,[38] the novitiate was opened for the coadjutor Salesians: a new Salesian presence of consecrated life designed for the world of work. In 1886, two years before Don Bosco's death, the basic document was drawn up which laid down the pedagogical, teaching and technical guidelines for the workshops. This document gathered together more than thirty years of educational experience of the saintly educator; thus this 'navigational chart' was intended to set out the fundamental guidelines for the development of future Salesian vocational schools.

The complete interpretation and implementation of the Salesian thinking and the necessary professionalisation progressively took place, taking into account the laws of the State and the encyclical *Rerum novarum* of Leo XIII (1891). At the seventh and eighth General Chapters (1895 and 1898 respectively), there was already talk not only of a basic intellectual training, but also of a professional culture. In the technical-vocational transformation, a number of initiatives were promoted: the development of curricula and the publication of texts and teaching aids; the organisation of professional and agricultural exhibitions; the serious and systematic preparation of management and teaching staff; the reconciliation of subject learning with the practical practice of the arts.

This development of the technical-professional field in the Salesian Congregation was, and still is, one of the most typical innovative expressions of Don Bosco's educational and pastoral thought. At his death, he left fifteen vocational schools; with his successor, Don Rua, they reached 88. In 1953, the first centenary of the Salesian professional schools, there were 263 (including the agricultural schools).[39]

---

38   *Archivio della Società Salesiana* (based in Rome), 0120. Don Bosco attended four General Chapters; the first was in 1877. We refer also to the documentation of J. G. González Miguel, *I quattro primi Capitoli Generali della Pia Società Salesiana, presieduti da don Bosco*. Ed. critica dei Verbali e delle Deliberazioni. (Madrid: CCS, 2016).

39   For a detailed study of the process of growth of the Salesian professional schools, see N. Zanni, 'Orientamenti e attuazioni delle scuole professionali salesiane', in Giraudo et al., *Sviluppo del carisma di Don Bosco fino alla metà del secolo XX. Comunicazioni*, 232–245.

3. Don Bosco's Writings and Youth Education

Placing the question of the Salesian educational-pastoral model in the broad context of Don Bosco's life, we can see how his profile as a writer is intertwined and identified with his peculiar educational style crystallised in an enormous literary production, both in terms of quantity and variety of writings.[40] This peculiar activity makes evident three aspects: a well-defined and visible organisational and educational physiognomy; a pedagogical experience embodied in reality; a remarkable flexibility in the progressive and coherent itinerary of its religious and civil activity (from 1845 to 1886).

Don Bosco communicated his projects in favour of the young people and the "pedagogy" that he practised with them. He addressed a wide and diverse range of people: collaborators, co-operators, benefactors; popes, cardinals, bishops, priests; kings, politicians, bankers, civil servants and administrators of state and local bodies. Without limiting his educational passion, he spared no effort in pooling his energies, making friends, finding new collaborators and seeking benefactors for his works in all social strata. To this end, he cultivated an abundant correspondence, a complex network of popular publications over a period of more than thirty years, as well as an extensive travel schedule in many cities of Italy and Europe.

1. His 'pedagogical narrative' forms an integral educational doctrine, which takes the form, among other things, of prolific correspondence with the public administration (official letters in which he illustrates the aims of his work and asks for material and moral help); in his writings addressed to his collaborators he publishes pages of a theoretical nature in which he tries to clarify the fundamental orientations of his action and summarise qualifying aspects of his system. He also reaches out to young people and the general public through a rich literary production of books and pamphlets, i.e., religious literature for young people and popular literature in the form of

---

40   Cf. P. Stella, *Gli scritti a stampa di S. Giovanni Bosco*, (Rome: LAS, 1977). Here you can read the complete list of titles and editions of printed material, classified into three groups: I. books and pamphlets; II. circular letters, programmes, appeals for help, testimonies, leaflets, posters; III. circulars, articles, texts of conferences published in the *Bollettino Salesiano*.

religious and civil history, biographies, short stories, Catholic apologetics,[41] pedagogy, catechesis, spirituality, dialogues and comedies. Finally, we must add numerous writings related to his role as founder and superior of religious and educational institutes (memoirs, constitutions and rules, etc.).

Despite this abundant literary dynamism, he never developed an abstract pedagogical hypothesis, a theoretical framework uprooted from reality; nor did he develop a systematic thesis in its theoretical, conceptual and epistemological aspects. He possessed pedagogical ideas and effective educational experiences, theoretical and practical approaches, the fruit of his experiential knowledge, typical of an educator on the street. His originality, therefore, is to be sought in praxis, in his daily work. His educational system is to be seen and experienced rather than to be contemplated perfectly in a framework of ideas and concepts. He was rather a man of action, and his essential principles on education were aimed at guiding educational praxis with young people.

He did not devote his life to being a theoretical and detached analyst of the prevailing physical, environmental or moral conditions of the time, nor did he get caught up in the complaints and grievances about young people: he was more concerned with solving the main educational problems that affected the lives of the poorest young people. This preferential treatment for the neediest young people came to be at the very centre of his heart; indeed, it was the criterion for analysing and validating the veracity and relevance of his entire educational model, of every project and initiative, of every educational and evangelising action.

He was always guided by real life experiences, which he subjected to a measured and continuous reflection. In order to reconstruct the praxis

---

41   This strong apologetic insistence is underlined in Don Bosco's writings. Proof of this is his famous collection 'Letture cattoliche', a form of apologetic prevention against Protestant and Waldensian proselytism, as well as the response to unbelievers. The fascicles of the first fifteen years show the main objective: the catechetical, religious and moral education of the people and of the young. Educational and catechetical intentions for young people and adults are also the series 'Vite dei papi', published between 1856 and 1865.

and pedagogical conception of Don Bosco in his many writings, we must also take into account his personal and institutional formation.[42]

Nevertheless, there is a guiding thread, an explicit 'discourse', an articulated reflection on education in his many written and spoken interventions. We can see a logical unity, a coherent pedagogical structure that allows us to outline some principles, criteria, suggestions, formative experiences, mistakes and errors from which to build an educational system.[43]

2. From the pedagogical point of view, the lack of books in the general community constituted a real difficulty. Don Bosco noticed this and immediately took on the task of preparing manuals and reading texts adapted to the ability of his boys "just as food must be allocated [according] to the stature of the individual."[44] Don Bosco's didactic competence in popular education was increasingly appreciated. His expertise was praised in manuals on the teaching of history, literacy, the teaching of arithmetic and the metric system ('*Il sistema metrico decimale ridotto a semplicità*', 1849) and the conversational catechetical method. Let us see an example when he narrates the dispute between Caesar and Pompey. In these words, there is the genius of educational thought:

---

42   The spirituality in which he was formed finds its roots in the seminary of Chieri, where he was from 1835 to 1841, and in the *Convitto Ecclesiastico* of Turin. For a synthesis of the spiritual context of his time, see Salesian Historical Institute, *Salesian Sources*, XXXIII–L.

43   "In the context of the works established, promoted and directed by him, he appears as a great educator. His personality, strongly rooted in the rural world of Piedmont, has attracted the attention of both pedagogues and, more generally, scholars of contemporary history. The development of Don Bosco's works was not merely the result of organisational skills and social situations that were well exploited. It was also the result of a lived pedagogy which, however it is judged, is coherent in its essential principles, and has been ductile in its development and in its application in changing historical situations. It was not a purely abstract idea, but the powerful spring of an educational relationship and of a complex system of works." (P. Stella, *Juan Bosco en la historia de la educación*. (Madrid: CCS, 1996), 33.). See also G. Avanzini, 'The pedagogy of St John Bosco in his century', in *Don Bosco in history*, 291–298.

44   This is the expression that Don Bosco himself writes in G. Bosco, *La storia d'Italia raccontata alla gioventù: dai suoi primi abitatori sino ai nostri giorni, con analoga carta geografica*. (Turin: Tipografia Editora Salesiana, 1882), 11.

As it was, Caesar and Pompey, the only leaders of the Roman Empire, fell into discord, because each wanted to hold on to power. At that time Caesar was in Gaul, and he and his army confronted Pompey, who was in Rome. You are surprised, young people, how two close friends became enemies and rivals so quickly. This happened because their friendship was based on ambition; and you should consider that true friendship cannot last unless it is founded on virtue.[45]

There was enthusiastic talk of his entertaining plays, comparative displays and Socratic method applied to the teaching of history. It was admired how, through the stage, song, gymnastics, music, fables and narrations, he spoke to his young people in their own language and reminded them of their hidden cultural roots.[46]

In as objective an understanding as possible, he shows us in the educational outline of his writings the reflection of his feelings and thoughts throughout the different moments of his life:[47] the *Memoirs of the Oratory of St Francis de Sales (1815–1855)*;[48] the biographies of Dominic Savio (1859), of Michael Magone (1861) and of Francis Besucco (1864), and other more or less

---

45   Ibid., 83. As can be seen, Don Bosco distinguishes and connects the learning of knowledge and its personal meaning, the didactic objective and the formative value, showing the educator that the academic discipline must be brought closer to the universe of the young.

46   To this are added books on human and civil education, such as *La forza dela buona educazione* and *La storia d'Italia*, and booklets oriented to religious, youth and adult education and formation, such as *La chiave del paradiso, Ritratto del cristiano, Il mese di maggio*, with the meditation on the '*Dignità del cristiano*', and the *Porta teco cristiano*

47   We refer to the scholars of Salesian studies that we find in the bibliography of this text: F. Peraza, *Iniciación al estudio de Don Bosco*. (Quito: Centro Salesiano Regional, 2003); P. Braido, *Prevenir, no reprimir: el sistema educativo de Don Bosco*.(Madrid: CCS, 2002); J. M. Prellezo (ed.), *Don Bosco en la historia*. (Madrid: CCS, 1990).

48   The *Memoirs of the Oratory of St Francis de Sales* were written by Don Bosco by mandate of Pope Pius IX in an autobiographical tone. They present with naturalness and narrative acuity those facts, adventures, counter events and providential events that took place at the beginning of his work. They can be considered the most original source for understanding Don Bosco's inspirations and educational orientations. [*MO*].

novelised lives;[49] the *Ricordi confidenziali ai direttori* of 1863; the last writings of 1885-1886: the *Testamento spirituale* and the three letters to the Salesians of America.

In summary, we focus on four categories of writings and documents that directly develop themes related to education:

• Short texts taken from books of the early years that underline his inspirations and principles, which would remain constant in the educational and pedagogical journey of Don Bosco: for example, the prologues of the *Storia ecclesiastica ad uso delle scuole* (1845), of the *Storia sacra per uso delle scuole* (1847), both considered books of narrative catechesis; also the prologue of '*Il giovane provveduto*', a proposal of Christian life for young people written in 1847 and which was the one that had the greatest editorial success.[50]

• Some initial overviews of "family pedagogy" referring to the first Oratory (for externs and for those received in the first orphanage); that is, three important narrative documents: *Regolamento per gli esterni,* which begins with the 'Introduction' of 1854, for the Oratory of St Francis de Sales; *Regolamento per le case della di S. Francesco di Sales,* which begins with the 'Piano di Regolamento' (Regulatory Plan) for the annexed house; *Cennostorico,* 1852-1854 and *Cennastorici,* 1862 (Historical background). The latter two

---

49   The biographies of Dominic Savio, Michael Magone and Francis Besucco are the narration of three boys educated directly by Don Bosco and in his works. The three biographies reflect the life of the Oratory in the decade 1854-1864, when Don Bosco was between 40 and 50 years old. They are the portrait of role models for educators and young people. It covers his educational conception and its finished realisation in three different types of boys. One is especially gifted and almost preserved from any external 'infection' (Dominic Savio); another comes 'from the street' and is transformed by education (Michael Magone); a third, with a natural disposition for good, who grows up in an educational environment with particular characteristics (Francis Besucco). See the introductory essay and the historical notes by Aldo Giraudo 'Masters and Disciples in Action' in G. Bosco, *Lives of Young People*, online: https://www.sdb.org/en/Don_Bosco/Biographical_Material/ Documents/Lives_of_Young_People__by_St_John_Bosco__Introduction_by_Ald [Accessed 24/06/2022].

50   In the year of Don Bosco's death, in 1888, it had reached its 119th edition. Cf. P. Stella, *Valori spirituali nel "Giovane provveduto", di san Giovanni Bosco.* (Rome: PAS, 1960), in which the spiritual life project proposed by Don Bosco to the young is described at length.

are two short manuscripts in Don Bosco's own handwriting in which he recounts, for the first time, the origin and development of his work.

• At the apex of Don Bosco's educational reflection are the texts on the Preventive System, from 1877 to 1878, which are to be considered classics.

• Another category of writings, the result of a collective and institutionalised tradition, are those closely linked to the personality of Don Bosco. They are his intuitions, but with formulations by others, the outcome of the community experience in Turin. The 'Circular on Punishments' of 1883,[51] not written by Don Bosco, but inspired by him and by the Oratory of Valdocco. The terms and concerns were Don Bosco's own at the time, even if the title itself is contradictory, given that the content is actually loving correction:

> I would also like to have a discussion, or rather a lecture, on the Salesian spirit, which must animate and guide our actions and all our words. The Preventive System must really be ours. Never harsh punishments, never humiliating words, never severe reprimands in the presence of others. On the contrary, let words of gentleness, charity and patience be heard in the classrooms. Never biting words, never a slap, neither hard nor light. Let negative punishments be used, and always in such a way that those who receive a warning are more of our friends than before and do not feel discouraged by us.[52]

To conclude: in these pages we have reflected on the pedagogical experience of Don Bosco, focusing on its characteristic traits that identify it in history. This reflection has allowed us to value the vocational sense of being a Salesian educator and to emphasise its anthropological, social and pastoral dimension, without which it would cease to be a Salesian approach.

---

51   Punishments were a customary pedagogical habit of the time, although they were beginning to be criticised. Don Bosco advocated the elimination of all physical punishment and the pedagogical use of 'moral' punishments: "For young people, anything that is made to serve as punishment... a serious look or the withdrawal of a token of trust is punishment."

52   Letter of John Bosco to Don Costamagna, August 10, 1885.

Chapter Three

Prevention Through Education: Guiding and Inspiring Principle

1. "A Grain of Sand" in Education

In this chapter we intend to explain the basic elements of the 'Preventive System', a principle that guides and inspires the educational-pastoral model. We will see how it is structured in the occupations of daily life, in the multidirectional relationships, in the priorities and in the design of all institutions, planning and projects.

The mission, vision and values framework that we have developed in Chapter 1 find their inspiration in the Preventive System, the expression used by Don Bosco to describe his spiritual and educational experience with the young

68

people of the Oratory, and which he recorded in a document of 1877 which he called a "little treatise". Here is an excerpt where his motives and intentions in writing it are evident:

> I have often been asked to give, either orally or in writing, some thoughts on the so-called "Preventive System" practised in our houses... I do this solely out of a desire to do my bit for the difficult art of educating young people. I will tell you, then, what the Preventive System consists of and why it should be preferred; its practical applications and its advantages... It consists in making known the rules and regulations of an institute and then watching over the pupils so that they always have the watchful eye of the director or of the assistants, who, like loving parents, speak, guide in every circumstance, give advice and correct with kindness; which is like saying: it consists in making it impossible for the children to indulge in misconduct.[1]

From the first experiences of his travelling Oratory to the consolidation of his work in Valdocco, Don Bosco harmonised and combined the various elements of his system and specified the reciprocal interdependence between the aims, the contents, the method, the style, the role of the educator and the characteristics of the educational institutions. Conscious of contributing "a grain of sand", he certainly has in view and admires the educational and pastoral experience of outstanding personalities of the Church: Saint Alphonsus, the Piarist Fathers, the Barnabite Fathers, Saint Philip Neri, St Francis de Sales, St Charles Borromeo, St John Baptist de La Salle and the Christian Brothers, among others. From all of them he intuits their fundamental components, takes them on board, adapts them and recreates them for practical and specific educational and pastoral action.[2] It is interesting to note how some ideas and educational practices were already formulated in the most influential authors

---

1   Salesian Historical Institute, *Salesian Sources*, 392.
2   Among the contemporary theorists of pedagogy recognised and highlighted by Don Bosco himself in his *Memoirs of the Oratory*, with whom he had cordial and friendly relations, we can identify the following figures: Abbé Ferrante Aporti (1791–1858), a famous figure of liberal Catholicism and a renowned educator who became rector of the University of Turin. His contribution to the concept of 'prevention' in education, among others, is highlighted; Giuseppe Rayneri (1809–1867), prestigious Turinese educator and professor at the Turin Athenaeum; Antonio Rosmini Serbati (1797–1855), priest, philosopher and one of the greatest Catholic theorists of nineteenth-century pedagogy.

of nineteenth-century Europe (Necker de Saussure, Lambruschini, Rosmini and, in particular, Pestalozzi).[3]

In his time, religious foundations dedicated to education had already arisen, which contributed to consolidating a preventive perspective in positive terms: the very term 'prevention' was not foreign to the pedagogical discourse or to the educational praxis of his time.[4] Prevention was related to the goals of education: to achieve good, virtue, the formation of honest and morally upright persons. In this context, the concept of 'educability' was also being constructed: an expression of the daily interpersonal dynamics between the learner and the teacher, where the goal was to lead the former towards perfection, personal growth, goodness and the truth. This contemporary thinking of Don Bosco also included the consideration of young people as having latent educational potential and not just a lack of it; he also believed in flexibility and personalisation in order to adapt to the individual, among other considerations.

Don Bosco knew how to gather and express all this with lucidity and skill in a new synthesis from which the Salesian pedagogical formula of the Preventive System in question would emerge: a regulating principle associated with his priestly soul, his educational attitudes and his practical choices. In this sense, it is reasonable to think that his very rich human and spiritual journey and his contact with reality would define his unmistakable stamp, which is grafted onto the vast history of Christian education with new personal reflections and realisations.

We present some topical elements of the Salesian educational system in order to offer the possibility of a comparative dialogue with the youth context in which we live. With the distance in time that separates us, it is amazing how current his intuitions resonate today, considering his time and ours. Certainly, the approach was created and put into practice in the nineteenth century, making it 'dated' according to and in conformity with those times that no longer exist; but it is always up to date, because it is 'translated' and

---

3   Other European educational representatives of the eighteenth and nineteenth centuries include Spencer, Canon Silvio Antoniano, Duvergier, Poullet, Dupanloup, Lacordaire, Monfat and Pavón.

4   See a synthesis of the pedagogical context in Salesian Historical Institute, *Salesian Sources*, XXII–XXXII.

decoded, inculturated and rethought in the light of modern educational problems, obviously unknown to Don Bosco. Today it continues to guide the educational-pastoral model, integrating and facilitating the development of the young and of all those who make up the educational-pastoral community.

2. The Preventive System: a Language with Different Emphases

Don Bosco's actions express his coherence with the practice of the founding principles described in the Preventive System. We can say that the 'genius' of his educational passion is linked to the implementation of a pastoral, educational and pedagogical system that is a model and inspiration for those who today are engaged in Salesian education on different continents, in multicultural contexts and characterised by religious plurality.

Salesian praxis has as its frame of reference and as a measure of authenticity the work of the Salesian Preventive System, which is a pastoral, spiritual and pedagogical proposal. A first step is to ask ourselves: what are the main points expressed in the terms 'system' and 'preventive'? Another step is to be aware of the profile and centrality of pastoral charity.

Later, in point 3, we will look into the pastoral content of the Preventive System as an educational project of integral promotion. Then, in this chapter, we will study the Preventive System as a suggestion of Christian life, a spirituality understood as a conscious journey made by the educator; in some way we can say that the system is first in the soul of the educator. The Salesian model solves the problem of the purpose of education in a clear and precise way: it does not conceive of a true education that does not focus on the whole person, as a person in this world in relation to God.

Finally, in Chapter Six, we will analyse the applications of the Preventive System as a practical method. We will examine its pedagogical evolution, closer to the specific educative-pastoral practice of the educator. This specific way of entering into relationship with young people and helping them to mature requires a series of resources and an understanding of youth psychology.

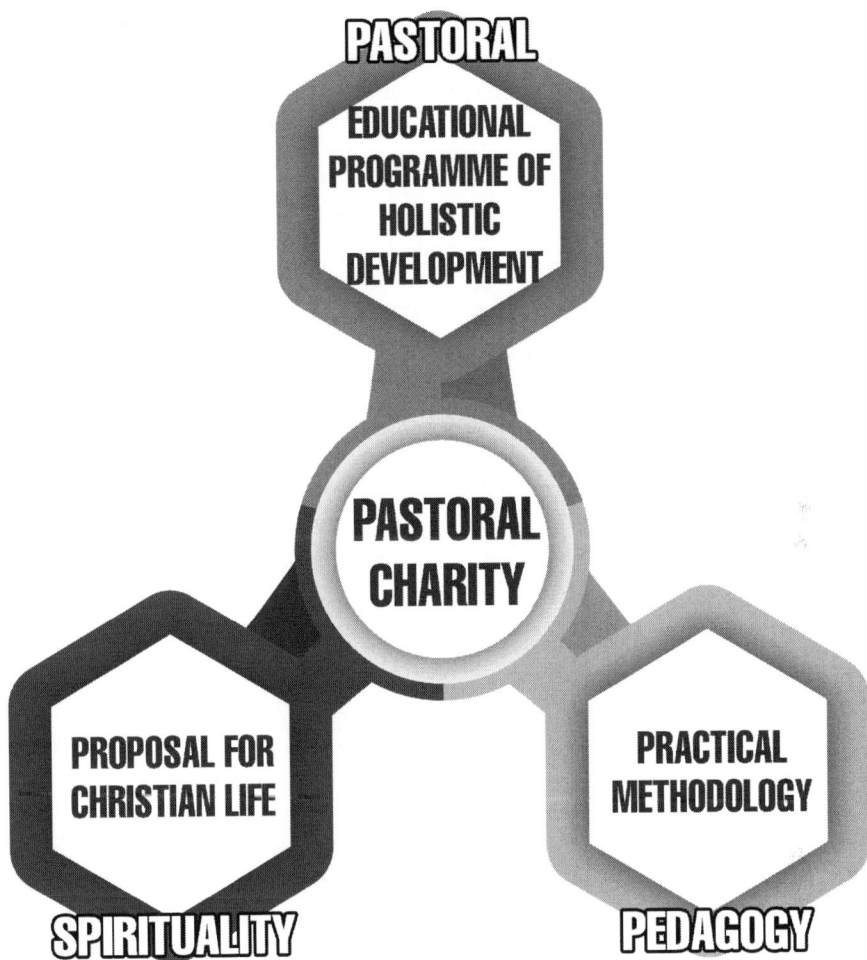

PASTORAL

EDUCATIONAL
PROGRAMME OF
HOLISTIC
DEVELOPMENT

PASTORAL
CHARITY

PROPOSAL FOR
CHRISTIAN LIFE

PRACTICAL
METHODOLOGY

SPIRITUALITY

PEDAGOGY

2.1. 'System' and 'prevention': an exceptional pairing

Regarding the first aspect, the word 'system' suggests the idea of wholeness, organic experience, dynamism, an articulated proposal of elements deeply linked to each other. Each one is a significant dimension of a broader educational proposal and, therefore, does not exhaust the richness and complexity of the whole. It refers, at the educational-pastoral level, not only to a broad vision with inspiring elements, but also to mechanisms, educational resources, methodological applications and their reciprocal interaction.

In the elaboration of this approach, the basic concept of 'prevention' must also be emphasised, which in the Salesian case does not focus primarily on socially privileged young people or on early childhood. It is aimed at adolescents and young people, who are always in need on a material, emotional, cultural or spiritual level. The passage of time has made it possible to discover its fuller and deeper meaning. The word has various meanings in general educational methodology, but in Salesian terms we can say that it is embodied in three preventive educational paths:

• The 'preventive criterion' aims to avoid harmful or damaging experiences in young people. It captures the more protective-negating meaning of the term, that particular sensitivity necessary in every educator to pay attention to anything that may constitute an irreversibly negative experience in a young person's developmental age. It is a matter of anticipating the risk factors to be combated or contained, of becoming aware of the risk of internal or environmental threats. In this case, prevention means reducing the incidence of evil, **avoiding, preventing, isolating, neutralising the negative and counterproductive elements**.

• On the other hand, it should be noted that prevention means bringing out the best in everyone, positively influencing the young person by promoting constructive and enriching experiences. In this way, it is not so much a matter of risk management, the aim is to promote and improve the person's starting conditions and resources. Thus, through sports, creative and cultural activities, among others, we activate their maturing process, their human potential, their opportunities to discover themselves and grow as a person. In this case, prevention means **promoting, empowering, building, reinforcing**.

• Finally, it also has a curative extension. Preventing here includes those interventions aimed at rehabilitating and recovering those who suffer complex, adverse or conflictive situations. It is, therefore, synonymous with **healing, shortening or lessening** the consequences of evil, slowing down the process of increasing vulnerability, preventing the definitive ruin of those who are on the wrong path, and doing so through education.

For Don Bosco's time, as in our own today, it is a question of the contrast between two different systems: the repressive and the preventive. Why repress if you can prevent? Why demand discipline if it is possible to adopt a kind and paternal practice?

2.2. Pastoral and educational charity

The ultimate foundation of the system is clearly theological, spiritual (cf. St Paul in 1 Cor 13: "Charity is kind and patient. It suffers all things, hopes all things, endures all things"), but it is also anthropological; that is, the preventive concern is elevated to a system of assistance, education and socialisation.

At the heart of this system is a certain spiritual attitude: pastoral charity. For Don Bosco, educating involves this special disposition of the educator, this deep-rooted conviction: to seek in a particular way the spiritual good of the young, their salvation, their integral good. Totally dedicated to his mission, he is ready to pay a price and to surrender everything: *Da mihi animas, coetera tolle* ("give me souls and take the rest").

In our opinion, this motto assumed by Don Bosco in the form of a prayer is the synthesis of his fundamental educational and pastoral choice. His whole life is focused on this approach, to see young people grow and mature towards their eternal destiny, understood in all its broad meaning. We can affirm that 'pastoral charity' is the specific educational-pastoral service of the Church that the Salesians offer to young people.

1. It might seem that the adjective does not add much to the noun. It should be noted, however, that the need for highlighting 'pastoral' indicates a form of charity, it reminds us of the figure of the Good Shepherd, his goodness, his search for the most distant and lost, his forgiveness, his revelation of a merciful God and Father. This 'charity that saves', the driving force of the Preventive System, reminds us that the source and the centre of the educational-pastoral experience is divine charity. We understand better how Don Bosco had this deep faith in the goodness and merciful Fatherhood of God. The very choice of St Francis de Sales as an example for his collaborators and as protector of his Congregation confirms this. His was an optimism rooted in the certainty that a providential God was guiding both the fate of the Church n what appeared to be extremely stormy times and also himself and his work.

2. Salesian pastoral charity has an original form that defines it best: it is an educational charity. It demonstrates affection, trust and love for young people. These three characteristics speak of the educational passion of the

one who dedicates all his time, but also of discretion, common sense, balance, affectionate collaboration and respect for the adolescent and the young person. It is a kind of 'pedagogy of incarnation' by means of which the personal and social history of the subject is taken care of in an educational way.

It is important to note that this affection, trust and love is the fruit of the conviction that every life, even the poorest, most complex and precarious, carries within it, through the mysterious presence of the Spirit, the power of redemption and the seed of happiness. An experience that recognises the dignity of every young person, renews confidence in his or her resources for good and educates him or her to the fullness of life. It aims, in short, at welcoming God in young people: in them God offers the grace of an encounter with Him and calls us to serve Him in them.[5]

The Salesian educator recognises the importance of the dignity of children of God and, at the same time, the fragility of a fickle and volatile age. We have always liked the image of the educator as a ships' captain, that is, one who accompanies from one shore (childhood) to another (adult life). But the journey is not linear: one paddles forwards, backwards and with unexpected turns. The ship is not meant to run along the coast and in calm waters.

It follows that a realistic view is required of the conditioning factors that can affect young people, some of them external (alienating situations, environmental influences, bad examples), others internal (uncontrolled inclinations, inadequate habits, poorly formed conscience, narcissism or simply disenchantment). For these reasons, all means must be brought into play and all ideal impulses, human and religious, immediate and supernatural, must be awakened.

It is also important to note that the Salesian educator believes that education prevents evil through an intangible value: trust in the good that exists in the heart of every young person. It is a matter of a charity called to open one's eyes and to look deeply. The educator must arrive with patience and respect at the place where young people's behaviour is born and takes root, their

---

5   Cf. General Chapter XXIII of the Salesians of Don Bosco, *Educating young people to the faith*, March 4–May 5, 1990. Online: https://www.sdb.org/en/ SDB_Resources/General_Chapters/CG23_(1990)/general_chapter_23 [Accessed 24/06/2022].

inner freedom, their own resources that need to be discovered, recognised and valued.

3. Pastoral-educational charity demands not only an affection for the young, trust in them and obvious love; it also activates a knowledge rich in humanity, a paternal wisdom. The term 'paternity' could be thought of as a simple, affectionate, rhetorical expression. In truth it is much more, it is the mature expression of pastoral charity; it leads the educator to seek only the good of the learner, forgetting himself completely and feeling strongly impelled to action and to a spirit of sacrifice.[6]

This mature and affectionate Salesian paternity makes the Salesian educator unmistakable in relation to the contemporary world, which is increasingly 'orphaned' and alone. According to the witnesses of his life, Don Bosco had a paternal kindness expressed in the form of innumerable kindnesses: expressions of loyal gratitude, invitations, small gifts, kind letters, gestures of interest, words of encouragement and of advice, the mere memory of which soothed hearts. Accusatory questioning, moralisation and the threat of blackmail were alien to him.

This adult paternity is expressed in the measure of the adolescent, who must be helped to open up, to discover the richness of life, to grow. The educator thus becomes a communicator of the Fatherhood of God: a charity that reaches the least, the humblest, and that wants to 'save', to elevate, to help them to take the next step.

As can be seen, this experience, at the same time spiritual and educational, possesses an intimate unity: to separate Don Bosco's pedagogical method from his pastoral soul would mean destroying both.

It is known for certain that this unity was translated into simple formulas in the words of Don Bosco, easily memorised formulas of synthesis within the reach of his boys, such as "health, wisdom and holiness"[7] of "joy, study,

---

6   It cannot be summed up better than in this phrase of Don Bosco himself: "I have promised God that even my last breath will be for my poor young people" *(BM,* XVIII, 258).

7   *Epistolario* VI. Introduction, critical texts and notes edited by F. Motto. (Rome: LAS, 1991–2016), 465.

76

piety"[8] or "bread, work, paradise".[9] He succeeds in uniting the essential and the unexpected of each day. For this reason, we can say that his educational programme, while being profound, is simple and within the reach of all; it is summed up by the binomial that Don Bosco presents as an inseparable unity: "honest citizens and good Christians", "to be an exemplary citizen because one is a good Christian",[10] in the words of St John Paul II. This proposal is the main expression and sign of identity of the Salesian educational-pastoral model.

4. The Preventive System is "the condensed pedagogical wisdom of Don Bosco and constitutes the prophetic message that he left to his own and to the whole Church."[11] For this reason it involves not only the educator, but also the community of which the educator is a part, together with and for the young people. In fact, in the practical commitment of a Salesian community or institution, every educational initiative is open with constant and competent understanding of the charity of the Good Shepherd: it is the 'methodological criterion' of the Salesian mission to accompany young people in the delicate process of the growth of their humanity in faith. At the same time, every spiritual dynamism of an educational community breathes an original approach to Christian life, organised around experiences of faith, values and evangelical attitudes that constitute Salesian youth spirituality, a theme that we will develop later.

8   *Opere edite* XV. (Rome: LAS, 1976–1977), 332–333.
9   *BM*, XVIII, 365; XVII, 220. For a study of this monumental work of nineteen volumes of the *Biographical Memoirs*, see F. Desramaut, 'How the authors of the Biographical Memoirs worked', in J. M. Prellezo (ed.), *Don Bosco en la historia*, 37–65.
10   John Paul II, Apostolic Letter *Iuvenum patris,* on the occasion of the centenary of the death of St John Bosco. (Rome, February 24, 1988), n. 10.
11   Ibid., n.8.

3. The Preventive System as an Educational Programme for Holistic Development

3.1. 'Educational charity' implies 'social charity'

Christian pedagogical humanism, on which the Preventive System is based, constitutes a welfare and social response that is at the same time educational and evangelising.

Don Bosco visited the prisons; he went through the streets and the workplaces to look for the boys. Even after the institutionalisation of the Oratory, he would send his Salesians to help the poor, abandoned and at-risk boys who were on the streets of Turin and who had no 'place' for their normal human and social growth. There are images that remained engraved on Don Bosco's mind and always accompanied him, such as that of that sea of faces seeking to be saved:

> Without taking into account many other expenses, the baker's bill alone for this quarter amounts to more than 1,600 francs, and I still do not know where to find a penny: and yet we have to eat; if I deny a piece of bread to these young people in danger and vulnerable, I expose them to a grave risk to their body and soul... It is not a question here of helping a particular individual, but of giving a piece of bread to young people whose need puts them in great danger of losing their morals and religion.[12]

As we saw in Chapter Two, Don Bosco's Oratory was born as a welfare and educational institution that offered quick and immediate answers to the poorest boys. In fact, the preventive praxis in its origins, even with different nuances, was composed of two inseparable activities, two ways of 'prevention':

• Satisfactorily meeting the primary needs of young people (food, clothing, shelter, security, work, physical and psychological development, social integration and life skills). This is what we can call 'preventive care'. Don Bosco discovered that young people lacked a father, a mother, brothers and sisters, affection, confidence and security. Many of them were illiterate, school dropouts, orphans, without a trade, with bad habits,

---

12   Letter of January 5, 1854: *Epistolario* I, 212.

surviving without being able to meet their most immediate and temporary needs: a roof to sleep under and a table to eat at.

• At the same time, it is a matter of giving life to an organic educational proposal, a harmonious and balanced formation that accompanies the intellectual, affective, social, physical and ethical-religious aspects of the person. We can call this action 'educational prevention' which contributes to each individual's growth in humanity.

This dual dimension of preventive education in the Salesian educational model (social assistance and education promotion aspects) is not chronologically separable in the actual and appropriate education of the young person.

We can already outline that the elements developed in this point, entitled 'The Preventive System as an educational programme for holistic development', reflects the concept that Don Bosco's 'preventive experience' is elevated to a 'system' of assistance, education and socialisation.

Educating means 'preventing' in all its possible meanings, i.e., helping each person to find themselves; accompanying with patience on a path of restoring values and confidence; it entails the reconstruction of reasons for living, discovering a new, more positive vision of existence, strongly anchored in what is essential for a better life. Educating also means a renewed capacity for educational dialogue, going beyond simple communication to become a rich source of interests. It involves engaging young people in experiences that help them to grasp the meaning of daily endeavours, providing them with basic tools to take charge of their own lives, enabling them to act as responsible citizens whatever the circumstances. Finally, educating requires an understanding of the social problems of the young people of our time.

3.2. The three pillars of the formative educational approach

Don Bosco's Preventive System can be summarised by kindness in relationships, educational reasoning and spirituality. This threefold view helps to understand its educational effectiveness. All educational and evangelising actions are imbued, explicitly and implicitly, with these three complementary views.

As has been pointed out, pastoral charity, the core of Don Bosco's educational system, is transformed, in the hands of the educator, into three pillars: 'reason, religion and loving kindness'. The basis of Don Bosco's pedagogy rests on this dynamism characterised by **the centrality of reason**, i.e., the rationality of the demands and norms, the flexibility and persuasiveness of the proposals; by **the transcendence of religion**, understood as the development of the desire for God inserted in every person and as the experience of assuming in this desire the beauty of the Good News; by the **urgency of loving kindness**, of the educational affection that makes one grow and generates reciprocity.

It is undeniable that the three elements interrelate with one another, both at the level of goals and content and at the level of methods and means. They are an original synthesis of the elements necessary for the holistic development of children and young people: physical, intellectual, moral, social, religious and affective. Methodologically, they activate a series of practical educational interventions to help young people develop their potential. We will develop this theme further in Chapter Six.

The three pillars are the fundamental inspiration of the educational approach for the development of the whole person; they give shape to a basic educational structure. In an attempt to synthesise them, the essential elements, which we consider valid and useful for the Salesian model, are presented below.

—**The catalytic principle of the method is love**. The Salesian name of pastoral charity is expressed in the so-called *amorevolezza* (loving kindness), the heart and soul of the Salesian spirit. A pedagogical love that is, above all, an authentic human love, an educational affection that makes relationships grow and generate reciprocity. Only such an affective bond makes 'familiarity' (a term adopted by Don Bosco and a trait inherited by tradition) possible,[13] helps to overcome individualism, self-absorption and self-referentiality. The justification of affectivity in education builds new relationships, new ways of being together, new times and new spaces. Therefore, *amorevolezza* is a form of affectionate friendship very dear to the Turinese saint, which is far from measured, formal and inflexible charity.

---

13   His statement is unusual and very enlightening: "Here, with you, I am at ease; my life is precisely to be with you" (*BM*, IV, 654).

1. It is not enough to just say that one is on the side of young people to really be on their side. It is necessary to love them with benevolence, respect, appreciation and recognition in their individuality and in their profound needs. It is a matter of taking particular care of the quality and authenticity of the communicative and affective relationship. What is sought is what the modern humanistic pedagogy considers authenticity to be a fundamental prerequisite for any formative process. With young people in particular, we cannot be inconsistent in what we feel, think, perceive and say.

It is important to emphasise that what is foremost in this special form of relationship is not the activity, but the presence "with and among" young people, aware that it is the strength of the free encounter that gives meaning to all the other values. It is a matter of personalising relationships against generalisation and simply providing services. But a second step is necessary: to arouse reciprocity, mutual love, affection freely given and returned.

Amorevolezza is a fascinating expression that gives special colour to the interrelational aspect of the educator and the young person. Of all the semantic echoes it raises, we will focus on the idea of fraternal and paternal friendship, affection given and received, the experience of love in relationship, a visible and perceptible love. In fact, a willingness on the part of the educator to welcome the young person cordially from his reality, and not in spite of his reality, should awaken in the young people the desire to express the best of themselves. A lot has been said about young people, but nothing has been said about the feelings that they evoke in each one of us and that we must know and respect. This love that we propose opens the heart and the intelligence of the young person to the educator, makes his suggestions and interventions friendly and stimulates his initiative and creativity.

The rediscovery of this requited love is the answer to the radical need of every person to "love and be loved": it is certainly one of the most influential factors in the approach and practice of the educational system of Don Bosco. As could not be otherwise, education is a matter of the heart: if the educator does not succeed in winning the heart of the young, their educational work is ineffective. This is a kind of 'master key' on which Don Bosco insists: do what young people love so that young people will do what the educator wants.

Psychological, historical and religious reasons led Don Bosco to the conclusion that education is the work of an essentially familiar educational structure. Exactly as in the family, the affective bond with each member is central. The magic of this educational style involves engaging in emotional processes, knowing that they are as important as rational ones, and that symbolic actions are as important as formal behaviours.

Loving kindness[14] was described by Don Bosco particularly in the Letter from Rome of 1884, of which we spoke in Chapter Two. It is a manifesto for educators because of its insistence on familial pedagogy, the atmosphere of affection, respect, socialisation, dialogue and trust.

He summarises what seems to him to be the cornerstone of the educational relationship, concerned with the improvement of the individual as a person. Don Bosco, mixing formulations of principles with facts and dialogues, with a strong emotional and colloquial tone, proposes a type of educational relationship and its personal and environmental expressions. This is nothing other than what he himself had lived and proclaimed in his life, in his action, in his educational work. This fundamental indication comes to Don Bosco from the childhood dream that determined the direction of his life: "Not by blows, but by gentleness, you must win these boys over."[15]

Referring to his own experience, he tries to make people understand that the willing love and the commitment of the educator is certainly something appreciable and good, but not enough and without pedagogical results if the young people do not 'feel' loved. Therefore, an educator who hands themself over completely to the young people but fails to make them feel that what

---

14   Jacques Schepens affirms that pedagogical love in the praxis of Don Bosco develops in three directions: loving kindness, loving-reason and loving-religion. Cf. J. Schepens, 'Dalle Costituzioni rinnovate: un nuovo orienta- mento per l'educatore salesiano', in Istituto di Spiritualità. Facoltà di Teologia dell'Università Pontificia Salesiana, Fedeltà e rinnovamento. Studies on the Salesian Constitutions. (Rome: LAS, 1974, 287).

15   When St John Bosco was only nine years old, he had a dream that affected him for the rest of his life. It would be the first dream-revelation that would mark the beginning of his mission among young people. In this dream he was invited to use gentleness to form those difficult young people into good Christians.

82

interests them is the person, will not achieve pedagogical results. In the words of Don Bosco:

Familiarity with young people is necessary, especially in recreation... Without familiarity, affection cannot be shown, and without this demonstration there can be no trust. He who wants to be loved must show that he loves.[16]

2. There is always an exchange of reciprocity, a flow in both directions. But it is also true that the formative relationship is always born of an asymmetrical condition (difference) that always saves it from a possible ambiguity that could contaminate the educational relationship. Emotional communication and the sharing of experiences must be well placed to allow growth of humanity in faith, in freedom, of both the learner and the educator. It must be a sincere love, befitting to those who are in contact with each other. The relationship is one that is both appropriate and constructive, without succumbing to emotional pressures or deception.

The demands of life are different and, consequently, so is personal maturity. The disparity is not absolute nor necessarily at all levels. It is a matter of promoting healthy, meaningful relationships where the educator is the one who must know how to model the different levels of communication and involvement.

Moving on in our reasoning, let us remember that Don Bosco knew the young people personally and knew how to speak to their hearts. His collaborators, adults and young people, were chosen with care for their personal gifts, their maturity and their level of integrity and spiritual life: they enriched the environment with their meaningful and friendly presence, with their pedagogy of love shown and received.

3. At present, as far as this first pillar of the Preventive System is concerned, we need only recall how the new educational theories grant the affective domain a vital importance in the formation of the individual as a human being; indeed, it is a component in the psychodynamics of the person that facilitates or hinders the very process of growth.

In short, the use of affection in education targets the construction of the complete human being, the integration of individual identities in all their

16   *Letter from Rome.*

complexity and beauty, sensitivity to mutual acceptance, tolerance and respect for others. Manifested love creates the person and unleashes the drive of growth towards maturity.

At this point, the Preventive System reminds us of the enormous restorative and transforming capacity of love, it evokes a complex reality embodied in attitudes, relationships, behaviour and feelings. In fact, it challenges the educator today in some pressing issues, such as the formation of conscience, education for love and the Christian view of sexuality.

—**Pedagogical love is also reasonable.** Pedagogical love must be accompanied by reason, i.e., it is a matter of appealing to the rational capacity to act in an informed way, to educate by means of a high level of pedagogical motivation with clarity of purpose and objectives. First in the educator, then in the young people. Each young person must understand what they have to do, grasped the importance of their motives and must be helped to remember them; only in this way can reasonable demands be made of them.

1. Hence the importance Don Bosco gave to regulations as a robust expression of values, of sensible agreements duly reasoned and explained. By adopting a method that organises discipline and interventions, he tried to humanise the young person through direct contact with values inspired by the realism of common sense: health, work, education, wholesome pastimes, good company and honesty. In the study carried out by Fr Braido on the regulations written by Don Bosco, he exposes the difference from those set out by other institutions: "The particular emphasis on humanity, gentleness and kindness, the singular attention to youth psychology, an important simplification of religious practices, the ample space given to play and recreation, the vividness of the feasts."[17]

Don Bosco attaches great importance to the human aspects and the psychological condition of the individual. For this reason, he calls for the educator to pay attention to the realm of what is realistically possible for a young person, of flexibility in dealing with situations, of adapting to the development of each person. Reasonable kindness manifests itself in many ways: demanding what is essential without complicating things; guiding daily

---

17   Braido, *Don Bosco The Young People's Priest In The Century of Freedoms,* I, 305.

life through clear goals, immediate and understandable gestures; helping to discern freely and responsibly; creating spaces for understanding, dialogue and patience, starting from an objective understanding of the individual in their circumstances and of the needs of the time; to promote a spirit of initiative, genuineness and spontaneity; to be bold in suggesting things in a reasonable and rational way, avoiding an unhelpful and soulless educational asceticism; to follow the method of early, calm, clear and sincere warning.

2. Reason becomes like the element that unites love and religion in the work of education, giving them reason, conviction and efficacy. This call to personal conviction, which is more practical than abstract, is based on an intelligently motivated persuasion, as opposed to constraint and imposition. It is that educational action which, on the one hand, reinforces motivational aspects, stimulating young people to develop their talents; on the other hand, it educates them not to rely solely on themselves and to avoid intellectual arrogance, servility or indifference.

Consequently, this pillar of the Preventive System is a call to every educator to educate in and for freedom and for the good. In a complex society, in which the capacity for judgment and a critical thinking are indispensable, reason presents itself as a magnificent terrain for educating in critical thinking and appealing to the cognitive capacity of the person, because those who know and can reason are able to see reality objectively and make free and responsible decisions.

The practice of educational reasonableness is also based on the goodness of the young people and on their openness to the truth. Don Bosco trusted his boys, he believed in their inner strength: it is precisely this trust in them that sustains his patience, his serene and vigilant optimism. It is a question of rejecting an approach that looks at young people only through a rear-view mirror, inevitably ending up by defining them in a negative way:[18] what young people do not know, do not do and are not. The reason is the tangible way in which Don Bosco lives humanism: young people who are poor and at risk, who suffer from the lack of many resources in their affective and psychological life, need the educator to believe in them, to know how to value them and to recognise their positive inner strengths in order to develop them.

---

18   Cf. B. Bellerate, 'Don Bosco and the humanist school', in *Don Bosco in history*, 317–332; A. Sopeña, 'A humanist model of Christian education', in *Don Bosco in history*, 515–522.

—**The religious question, the unifying aspect of the whole system**. Don Bosco, the founding father of orphans, mature educator, dreamer and daring entrepreneur, intuitive promoter of pastoral and educational initiatives, can be understood from the two dynamic nuclei of his vocation: on the one hand, a cordial and affectionate attitude towards young people, and, on the other, the unconditional gift of self to God as a response to the mission received. For Don Bosco, cordial and reasonable love is nourished by a deep rootedness: he felt himself to be a friend among the boys and always a priest.

Pedagogical love for children and young people is enlightened by religion, i.e., by the development of the desire for God innate in every person. Don Bosco's pedagogy is constitutively transcendent in that it harmoniously unites the human and the divine, bringing to the fore the beauty and fullness of the moment in which these two dimensions meet. It is only from this desire that religious interest is aroused, and the graciousness of God's gift freely given is discovered. It is a matter of opening oneself to the surprise, of tasting the 'flavour' of the things of God. The notion of religion as the foundation and crowning glory of a successful education is essential in understanding our model.

In fact, a faithful reading of the Preventive System reveals the humanistic richness and the fundamentally religious heart of the system. A young person's character is not reduced to a simple 'human condition' making them no longer a child of God. It can thus be argued that the religious question is a unifying aspect of the whole education system and, at the same time, an educational task to accompany the whole of life.

We can therefore affirm that for the Salesian, educational love is a sign in itself of God's love for young people. If He is the source of optimism, He will not allow us to fall into pessimism and let ourselves be discouraged by difficulties! Faith helps us to discover the religious scope of problems, insecurities, the desire to live and to be happy. For Don Bosco, the last word is always on the paternity of God, on His goodness, on the maternal protection of the Virgin Mary, on the reassuring and purifying power of reconciliation, on the joyful encounter of communion. Paradise clearly dominates the spiritual horizon, where everyone will find his or her own 'home'.

1. The difference between a generic religious faith and the Christian faith lies in the recognition of Jesus Christ, God's definitive witness. It is therefore the religion of the good news of the Gospel, of the Beatitudes, of Jesus, who considered his disciples friends and not servants, and who calls everyone to seek the Kingdom of God and His justice. The religion of the Preventive System awakens a sense of wonder, is popular, simple and goes to the heart of the matter: "love of God and love of neighbour". The commandment of love is unique, but at the same time it has two points of reference, God and neighbour. It inspires a simple and joyful spirituality because it is open to all; it is attractive because it is charged with human values, and for this reason it is particularly appropriate for educational action.

More precisely, it is the religion of the devout humanism of St Francis de Sales, who learned from God to be kind, good, capable of patience and forgiveness; and in the incarnation of the Lord, recognises that we are all called in the Son to share in holiness, to live according to the Gospel in every condition of life, at every moment, in every situation, in every age. As can be seen, the apostle of kindness inspires the intentions of the priest Don Bosco.

Within a global programme of humanisation, the Salesian programme directs the person to maintain a dialogue with God in order to know, love and listen to Him. Don Bosco's holiness is materialised in his great educational passion: he lived his mission as an educator with a deep apostolic heart and proposed holiness as the ultimate goal of his teaching; he was also convinced that a true education is not possible without having as an end point the inner world of the person, their transcendent dimension and their eternal destiny.

Don Bosco would not be understood without the religious soul of his pedagogy. The educational purposes are not purely humanitarian or social, but also evangelising. We would be missing the historical point if we were to consider the Oratory conceived and set up by Don Bosco as a simple recreational space, a joyful and busy meeting place for young people. He wanted this institution to consider the final goal as the Christian religious element: a Sunday meeting house where everyone could have the best conditions to carry out their religious duties and, at the same time, receive instruction, guidance and good advice for life. Moreover, when Don Bosco speaks of religion, he does not reduce it only to the Oratory, but presents it as the basis for the formation of every person. We see this when he says: "Religion is capable of beginning and accomplishing the great work of a true education."[19]

2. It is a matter of presenting the life of a believer as an integral and achievable ideal: the time for inner search and religious practice that is proposed to the young person must be 'reasonable' and offered in a rational way. Faith gives a component of coherence in life; it is not a tool for indoctrinating others. Evangelisation is always closely integrated with human development and with the freedom of the Christian faith.

For his part, Don Bosco matured the conviction that with goodness and reason, rather than with rigour, it is possible to attract people, especially the young, to the practice of religion and Christian life. He judged that, outside of this perspective, the educational approach lost its strength and meaning. Young people, who are also called to the real fullness of life, communion with God and with their neighbour, need other strategies.

Without rejecting the primacy of the mystery of God, faith rests on the understanding of what is exposed and adapted. The 'religion' of the Salesian educational system promotes a faith that is sufficiently knowledgeable about religious culture; in fact, Don Bosco's first works for young people are publications on religious culture, sacred and ecclesiastical history, apologetics and asceticism.

3. Today, in an age of educational urgency, this educational passion fulfils a mission capable of achieving highly satisfactory results. Even in secularised contexts where the culture is incapable of speaking of the Father of Jesus Christ, it will be necessary to educate a sense of transcendence and to give answers to the great questions about the meaning of life and death, of pain and love, without hiding the ray of light that comes to us from religious faith. The marginalisation of religion in the lives of young people is not only the result of secularisation or indifference, but also proof of the high degree of uncertainty and fear associated with adhering to a particular creed and assuming a committed lifestyle.

In the great monotheistic religions, the first educational dialogue is with those young people closest to us in order to recognise together the grace present

---

19   *BM*, III, 463.

in them, to stimulate the desire for prayer and to value the fragments of the Gospel and of educational wisdom present in the culture, life and experience of the young people themselves.

4. The Preventive System as an Original Approach to Spirituality

4.1. Salesian spirituality, a tangible expression of pastoral charity

After looking at the essential components of the Preventive System as an approach to holistic development, we will discuss other features that also constitute it: we refer to the Preventive System as a programme of Christian life and a path of spirituality.

Spirituality is the fundamental basis and end point that gives meaning to Christian existence. The implementation of the Preventive System suggests a spirituality that favours a unifying vision of life, indicating the close and innate bond that embraces the graciousness of God, the joy of the encounter with Christ and the freedom of life in the Spirit.

1. To refer to spirituality is to refer to Christian identity and holiness: these are realities that are deeply intertwined to the extent that they identify with each other. A mature believing individual will be a spiritual person who reaches maturity when being in the presence of God becomes as natural as breathing, sleeping or thinking. Basically, it is a vitality that touches not only the religious life but the whole of life, determining in many cases the fundamental choices of the spiritual person. Spirituality is a rereading of the Gospel capable of unifying the actions and attitudes that identify and characterise Christian existence. It is something that identifies all the disciples of Jesus.

Inner life means to possess within us a certain movement that makes us think, speak, study, act and love in a particular way. It moves us from within ourselves and places us outside, in the face of reality, in order to question and analyse it. We try to shed light on the most elementary situations of the inner life, attempting to grasp the dynamics of the growing subject.

To specify what kind of interiority we are talking about, we refer to the interior life inhabited by the Spirit, which has to be lived in the exercise of the theological virtues of faith, hope and charity. It implies placing one's whole reality in God's orbit.

2. Christian spirituality is nourished by the message of the Gospel, despite there being different types of Christian spirituality, according to significant historical and, above all, charismatic nuances. All these are discovered in the Trinitarian experience of God, on a personal or community level. In the ecclesial tradition, the various founders, enlightened and guided by the Spirit, have strongly emphasised some evangelical values.

In his pedagogical and pastoral experience, Don Bosco revealed the path of youth spirituality and painstakingly demonstrated the validity of its great purpose with admirable results. Many testimonies in history and in the present-day bear witness to this. This is illustrated by those young people of Valdocco who achieved a truly exemplary lifestyle from the spiritual point of view.[20]

His is an educating spirituality: the secret of his success is his intense pastoral and educational charity, that inner energy that inseparably united in him the love of God and the love of young people. From a Christian perspective, this zeal for the most neglected young people in the various forms of poverty in which they find themselves, is an expression of the saving will of God incarnated in the figure of the Good Shepherd, who knows each one, who calls them, by their own name, and goes out to meet them.

The Church recognises that Don Bosco's reading is authentic and, for the avoidance of doubt, declared him a saint. His dedication to young people does not mean that he put all his efforts into only working with young people. Nor does it mean that his first concern was his own salvation; perhaps the most important thing is that, in giving his life to young people, he became a saint: the essence of his life was rooted in a living spirituality that nourished him and impelled him to seek God by serving young people.

Within this rationale, Salesian spirituality involves everyone: Salesians, lay people involved in the spirit and mission of Don Bosco, family and young people; it is called the 'Oratorian heart'. In other words, courage, apostolic zeal,

20   Cf. Bosco, *Lives of Young People.*

development of all personal resources, search for new actions, ability to endure trials, willingness to start again after failures, mature and infectious optimism.

4.2. Programme and path of Salesian youth spirituality

The spirituality that we propose here is adapted to young people, it is lived with and for young people, it is thought out and realised within the experience of the young person. Its aim is to generate a Christian life that can be offered to any young person who, in today's world, wants to walk a Christian path.

The following five elements are mutually interwoven; each represents an importance that reinforces what has been expressed in the others. They are points of reference which unify all Christian life:

• **Everyday life** as the most suitable place that God provides for us to meet Him, and in this way to grow and fulfil ourselves as individuals.

• **Joy** as an outward expression of the happiness we experience when we feel good with God, with others and with ourselves.

• The **Risen Jesus Christ**, companion on our journey and model of humanity, with whom we are called to establish a profound relationship through the Word, prayer and the sacraments, especially Reconciliation and the Eucharist.

• **Church-community** of all those who live according to the way of Jesus and make it a reality by being active and responsible members. Mary, the woman full of life, the first believer, who collaborates with Christ in the work of salvation, encourages and helps us as mother and teacher.

• **Commitment** as a responsibility to assume the task of collaborating in the construction of a more humane and just society, in the light of Gospel values, with a particular concern for the poorest young people.

—**Daily life as a place of encounter with God**. One cannot be a spiritual person by running away from the daily grind or by simply 'doing spiritual things'. Salesian youth spirituality considers daily life as a place of encounter with God, it does not separate personal and collective everyday life from the experience of faith. At the root of this perception of daily life and of the positive evaluation of life is the presence of the God of Jesus and the constant understanding of Incarnation: a spirituality that allows itself to be guided by the mystery of God, who with his incarnation, death and resurrection affirms his saving presence in the whole of human reality.

According to Don Bosco, to become a saint it is necessary to do 'well' what must be done: he considers fidelity to one's daily duties to be a criterion for verifying virtue and a sign of spiritual maturity. His call to holiness for young people is fully in line with the desire to live and the search for happiness, but also with the practical realism of each day, linking it to one's duties as a student (or worker) and as a good Christian. In other words, Salesian spirituality does not shy away from the present, it does not renounce the practicalities of life.

From the above we can understand why Don Bosco offered his young people an easy and joyful holiness. He revealed a daily life that was to be undertaken, deepened and lived in the light of God. It is a matter of reading into the daily events, contemplating the commitment to others, the tension of growth, family life, the development of one's own abilities, the prospects for the future, the daily demands and aspirations of life. It is in daily discourse and everyday life that the person reformulates his or her intentions, changes the way he or she looks at reality, raises questions, explores his or her own limits, is born to compassion, is shaped as a person in process... always in the light of God's kindly gaze.

It should be noted that the ideal of Salesian holiness is not reserved to a few; it has always been addressed to all without exception. In fact, there are countless young people and adults who have offered a fresh, hopeful and provocative reading of the Gospel. Likewise, many Salesian educators show the closeness of God. Rereading their lives, it is always a source of great admiration to find joyful souls who, without compromise, one can trust and imitate. They are the richest encyclopaedia in which to read the Preventive System of Don Bosco. A gallery of young people and educators that represents only a part of the catalogue of immense and varied human richness that this spirituality has produced.

For daily life to be lived as spirituality, a unified vision is needed, a harmony that orchestrates life around a heart inhabited by the Spirit of Love. This 'grace of unity' makes conversion and purification possible; it works in such a way that, through ordinary work and inner life, the heart remains free, open to God and dedicated to others.

92

—An Easter spirituality of joy and optimism. The spirituality that is suggested is marked by joy; it is its primary fruit. It is also the noblest expression of happiness and one of the richest elements of Don Bosco's pedagogy, together with celebrations. "Serve the Lord with gladness" (Ps 100:2) is the biblical phrase found among the first lines of Don Bosco's work '*Il giovane provveduto*'.[21] Salesian joy is love enjoyed, the greater the love, the greater the joy.

But this element connected to religious experience does not represent a concession (nothing looks so false as the behaviour of those who are cheerful out of obligation), but rather a consequence: joy is the expression of inner peace, it is the perfect antidote to sadness in all its forms; it indicates harmony with oneself, something that can only derive from being in harmony with God and with His creation. It has, therefore, ethical and religious implications.

Don Bosco sees in it an indispensable manifestation of the life of grace. For Christians of all times, believers of every age, race and condition, their vital joy is the result of a serene heart in the encounter with God.

For Don Bosco, this is the joy of "let nothing disturb you".[22] He passed on to his young people and educators that we believe in a God who cannot contain His joy at the happiness of His children, and who, therefore, neither desires nor expresses anything else but that we, too, overflow with joy. This is how Salesian joy is not an unimportant attitude: paradoxically, it is not usually seen in flashy things, it does not make noise, it is not extravagant.

This is why he invited his boys to explore new paths, to value daily events as positive, full of trust in the Father; this is the reason for Dominic Savio's famous expression: "Here we make holiness consist in being cheerful." Don Bosco understood, and helped his young people understand, that commitment and joy go together, that simple holiness and joy are inseparable.

—A spirituality of friendship and personal relationship with Jesus. Salesian youth spirituality leads the young person to an encounter with Jesus, making a relationship of friendship with him possible, nourished by trust and sustained by faithful devotion. Many young people feel a deep desire to know Jesus and

---

21   Bosco, *The Companion of Youth for the Practice of Religious Duties*.
22   Taken from *Prayer of St Teresa of Ávila* (1515–1582).

seek an answer to questions about the meaning of their lives, an answer that only God can give.

According to the Salesian approach, 'Friend', 'Master' and 'Saviour' are the names that describe the importance of the figure of Jesus in the spiritual life of young people. It is interesting to remember that Don Bosco presents Jesus as a friend of the young, present in the little ones and in those in need; as a teacher of life and of salvation; as a model for every Christian; as a redeemer who gives his whole life in love and in passion for salvation, even unto death. He would frequently quote Matthew: "Whenever you have done these things to one of the least of these my brothers or sisters, you have done it to me" (Matt 25:40).

—**A spirituality of ecclesial and Marian communion.** The experience and the appropriate understanding of the Church are hallmarks of Salesian spirituality. The Church is a spiritual fellowship and a community made visible through actions; it is service to people, from whom it is not detached; it is the place chosen and offered by Christ, in the time and space of history, in order to be able to meet him. He gave the Church the Word, Baptism, his Body and Blood, the grace of forgiveness of sins and the other sacraments, the experience of communion and the power of the Spirit, which lead to charity towards our brothers and sisters. Salesian youth spirituality seeks an increasingly responsible and courageous sense of belonging to the local and universal Church. In fact, the family of Don Bosco preserves, among the treasures of its home, a rich tradition of filial fidelity to the successor of Peter, and of fellowship and collaboration with the local Churches.

—**Salesian youth spirituality is a Marian spirituality.** God the Father called Mary to be, with the grace of the Holy Spirit, Mother of the Word and to give him to the world. The Church looks to Mary as an example of faith: Don Bosco also looked to her in this way, convinced that the Holy Spirit gave rise to the Salesian work, with the intervention of Mary, as article 1 of the Constitutions of the Salesians of Don Bosco says: she indicated to Don Bosco his field of action among the young, she led him and constantly supported him, she is present today and continues his mission as Mother of the Church and Helper of Christians. Salesian spirituality also recognises her as the Immaculate, wholly available to God, full of grace and holiness.

In the Oratory of Valdocco, Mary was a living presence: the inspirer, the guide, the teacher. Dominic Savio, Michael Magone and many other young people did not contemplate an abstract or a simple object of culture and devotion, but a person living and working, filling the house and making people feel and experience the closeness of God's love. Salesian youth spirituality encourages a simple and trusting entrustment to the maternal assistance of the Virgin Mary, the help of Christians in the great battle of faith and in the building of the Kingdom of God, the one who protects and guides the Church. She sustains and supports the faith, considered by Don Bosco as 'Our Lady of difficult times'.

In Mary Help of Christians, we find a model and a guide for educational and apostolic action. It is proposed that we imitate her with love and admiration, participating in the celebrations in her honour and remembering her as her children.

—**An apostolic spirituality at the service of the good**. Don Bosco sensed the enormous spiritual tension and the extraordinary apostolic force that the missionary ideal awakened in many people. He grasped it and used it with ardour and intelligence. It was the realisation that everyone in the world has a place and that everyone's gifts are needed, that life contains within itself a vocation to service. Salesian youth spirituality, therefore, wants to help each young person to place themself in a new inner (vocational) dimension, so that they can discover their place in history and their truth in dialogue with God. This finds strong support in the apostolic experience of the young Don Bosco. Starting from the dream of the age of nine, he understood and lived his existence as a vocation, listening and responding with a generous heart to an invitation: to be present among the young in order to save them.

As we have seen, a reading of Don Bosco's life reveals a fine sensitivity in perceiving the situations in which young people lived, a realism in providing valid solutions, both immediately and in the long term, and a capacity to position his educational initiatives with a view to the future and the transformation of society. He brought his solutions to social and educational problems from a Christian humanist point of view, i.e., by developing to the full the practical exercise of love for one's neighbour. He intuited that, in the face of the new times, new criteria for educational work and new ways of being present in the world were needed.

For this reason, Salesian youth spirituality is apostolic: it has the conviction that we are called to collaborate with God in His mission, with dedication, trust, availability and a critical sense of social reality for the building of the Kingdom. It is a real commitment to the selfless service of the good. It is not, therefore, a spirituality of relaxation or of peaceful equilibrium. Rather, it is a spirituality that makes young people evangelisers of other young people with an educational spirit, pastoral skills and apostolic passion.

Young people are not treated as mere recipients of the initiatives proposed by educators, but as partners. Don Bosco immediately sought out positive leaders; he tried to win their friendship and offered them the chance to be better; and he launched them in the midst of their companions with these words: "Seek to do them good". For this, both then and now, it is necessary to teach the ability to discern, to dissent, to choose, to opt, to decide, to cooperate and to take charge of reality: of oneself, of others, of history and of the environment. The novelty of Don Bosco's pedagogy lies in an educational approach that is both personal and group-based, and also religious and civic.

The spiritual, moral and religious dimension of humanity finds in faith the dynamism that makes it a reality in works, in commitments, in authentic testimonies of solidarity with others; in short, it is a question of shaping people and transforming the world. Apostolic work and educational commitment, personal formation and the building of society are united in this spirituality.

In short, the Salesian educator realistically appreciates and values the interests and needs of young people, as well as their shortcomings and strengths, their moral excellence and their flaws, their weaknesses and their ingenuity. And with all this, new generations are aroused, involved and directly committed, they become architects of the future, ready to work together in the construction of a society, to train them for the practical meaning of social life.

96

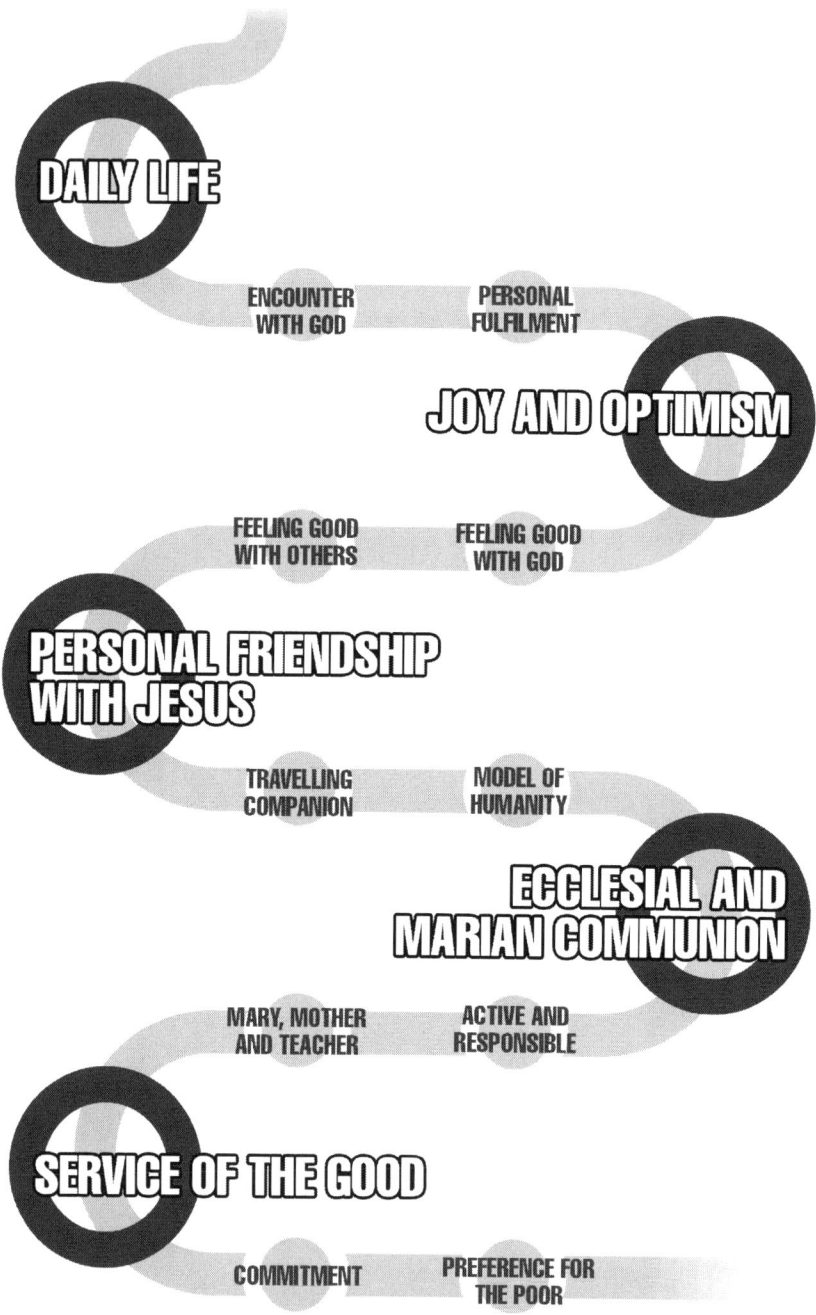

DAILY LIFE

ENCOUNTER WITH GOD

PERSONAL FULFILMENT

JOY AND OPTIMISM

FEELING GOOD WITH OTHERS

FEELING GOOD WITH GOD

PERSONAL FRIENDSHIP WITH JESUS

TRAVELLING COMPANION

MODEL OF HUMANITY

ECCLESIAL AND MARIAN COMMUNION

MARY, MOTHER AND TEACHER

ACTIVE AND RESPONSIBLE

SERVICE OF THE GOOD

COMMITMENT

PREFERENCE FOR THE POOR

Chapter Four

The Educational-Pastoral Community: Subject and Scope of the Salesian Approach

1. The Salesian Spirit: Community Experience

The main value of the educational-pastoral model lies with its participants. Each Salesian work is configured as an 'educational-pastoral community' made up of a group of people who relate, interact, share and enrich each other for the benefit of the defined common project. This community or group of people is the subject and, at the same time, the object and scope of educational and pastoral action.

The first fundamental element for the implementation of the Salesian educational-pastoral approach is a community, a group that includes young people and adults, parents and educators, together in a family atmosphere. The Preventive System, attentive to the personal relationship, is also community-based: it is inclined to bring people together in the service of the same mission. The educational-pastoral model that we are developing here is corporate, not individual. It requires the innovation and goodness of the whole group of people, their opinions and differences, the balance of different sensitivities and resources

1.1. The Salesian way of being present among young people

A fundamental task of the educational-pastoral community is to collaborate in the development of the formative development: the Salesian educational-pastoral project. It is not a new enterprise. It is much more. It is the convergence point of all activity; it implies the challenge of changing the mindset[1] in terms of the way of thinking, of evaluating and of acting in a co-responsible way; it implies facing not only the organisational task, but also the style of relationships with the young people and among adults that this entails; it involves everyone in an effort to build something new. It implies an adequate articulation and programming of interventions, always looking for coherence between what is desired and solid practices. Without a project, only urgent matters are attended to.

1. Salesian institutions accompany an enormous number of children and young people with complex needs; they offer creative and therefore risky responses consistent with the times in which they are living. Thanks to the project, educators establish a commitment to the goals, they concentrate on the means that lead to them and they are obliged to ensure the necessary conditions to achieve them. A school is 'Salesian' not because everything revolves around Don Bosco, but because of its educational-pastoral strength. This means, first of all, that it has an educational soul in its practices and in its

---

1   Prof. Michal Vojtás, professor at the Salesian Pontifical University of Rome, proposes six procedural virtues that summarise the balances that must be put in place in personal and community work according to an educational-pastoral project. Among the personal virtues, he points out creative fidelity, personal discernment and operative coherence. As prosocial virtues, he points out three others: systemic generosity, generative dialogue and synergistic integration (cf. M. Vojtás, 'La componente metodologica per l'educazione salesiana attuale', in V. Orlando (ed.), Con Don Bosco, educatori dei giovani del nostro tempo, 141–142).

ability to review and plan the education of the new cohorts. It implies a new way of looking at things that allow us to dream, that unites us with others.

On another level, a Salesian institution understands evangelisation as the fruit of a collective journey, joining forces to collaborate in the exchange of ideas, even with differences in training, tasks, charisms and degrees of participation in this mission. In this community, all are co-responsible, consecrated and lay, active subjects and builders of a future. What could be expected from a group of equals? Only equal answers. Therefore, the model we propose consists of a real, active and organised partnership where everyone contributes ideas, experiences, messages or decisions. Individual responsibilities are recognised and undertaken by all. The coexistence, the knowledge of teamwork, the shared educational-pastoral intelligence is greater than the sum of the individuals.

2. Recalling the beginnings of Valdocco, we have found the pastoral heart of Don Bosco, capable of involving the young people themselves in service: church, classrooms and playgrounds become educational realities thanks to the support of clerics and lay people, aware of a delicate and demanding undertaking that requires effort and collaboration.

The crucial role played by the laity since the beginning of the Oratory is a clear sign that the Salesian model believes in the importance and significance of their leadership, taking advantage of, encouraging and accompanying their skills at the service of a project that transcends the scope of their individual interests. In a Salesian school, for example, lay teachers bring their experience of lay Christian life, expressing it culturally and professionally in life choices, knowledge and practical activities, including in the various extracurricular and formative initiatives. It is unthinkable today to do without the diversity of vocations.

We can say that this scenario, characterised by an approach of educational co-responsibility of different vocations, is the clearest sign of the educational-pastoral community. Working together makes sense not only from the operational and functional point of view, but also from the point of view of witnessing pedagogy. In a society where solitude and extreme individualism is spreading, our way of educating and evangelising is the fruit of the convergence of consecrated and lay people, with a shared purpose and cultivated with mutual understanding.

This is why it is necessary to structure and give form to this coordination by creating the corresponding bodies. Formal involvement alone can lead to disinterest and to a certain 'absenteeism'. Participation, not only by sharing objectives but also values, is a process as well as a product, given that it achieves a strong sense of belonging to the group and to the educational project that must be carried out together. Achieving this generalised conviction of common objectives and responsibilities will lead to a feeling of ownership of the local problems, to taking an interest in its actions, to maintaining close relationships among all participants, to contributing one's own possibilities for acquiring experience.

3. The educational-pastoral community is the Salesian way of being present among young people. It is not just a group of people concerned with the education of young people; it is also the Salesian style of animation of each educational situation. It is not a new structure to be added to other existing management agencies or organisations, nor is it a tactic to better organise the work or increase participation. Let us explain the content of each of its terms:

• **community**, because it involves young people and adults, parents and educators in a family atmosphere, where the fundamental element of unity is not work or efficiency, but the harmonisation of vital values that make up a shared and loving identity;

• **the educational approach**, because it places the concern for holistic development of young people at the heart of their projects, relationships and organisations, addressing all aspects of their growing potential;

• **pastoral ministry**, because it is open to evangelisation, walking with young people towards an encounter with Christ and creating a Church experience where, with young people, the values of human and Christian communion with God and with others are experienced.

1.2. The educational-pastoral community, an intergenerational reality

1. Education is becoming more and more complex because of the fact that we live in environments: children, young people and adults pose new challenges to educational action. In any case, it is a community structured in concentric circles, in which the young people, the fundamental point of reference, are at the centre; the Salesian religious community, guarantor of

the Salesian identity, core of communion and participation; the families, first and foremost responsible for the education of the young; the laity in general, leaders, collaborators and the greatest possible number of people interested in the social and religious aspects of the Salesian approach.

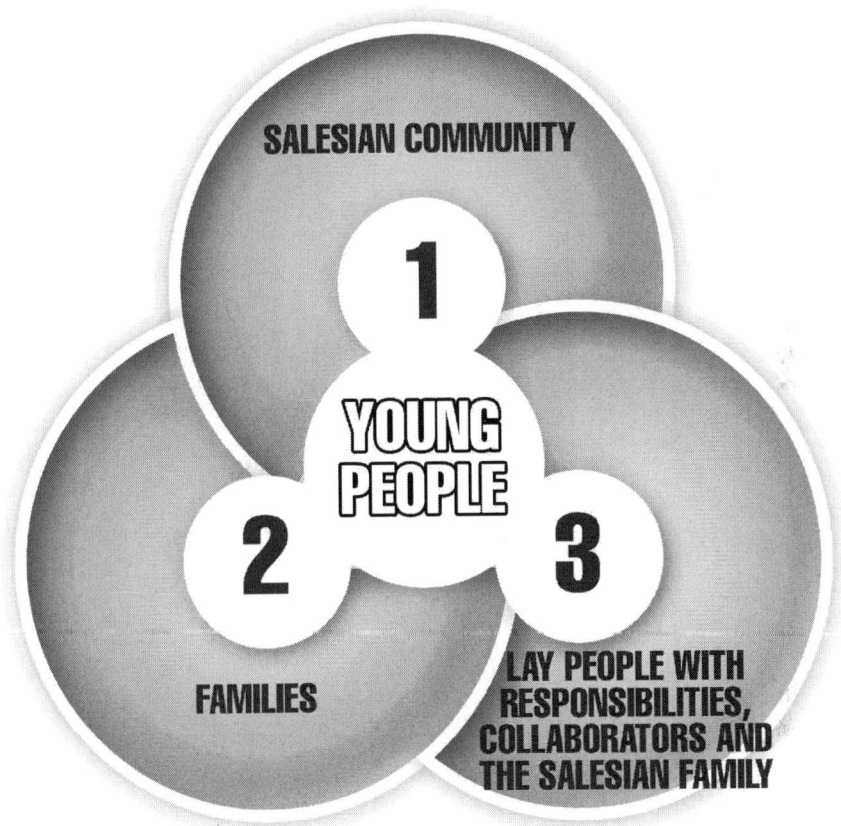

SALESIAN COMMUNITY

1

YOUNG PEOPLE

2   3

FAMILIES

LAY PEOPLE WITH RESPONSIBILITIES, COLLABORATORS AND THE SALESIAN FAMILY

The most significant educational-pastoral initiatives are interconnected like a network, typified by the Salesian oratory-youth centre, for example. It is the presence of adults who share with young people an atmosphere of friendship, an educational approach to life and an experience of family and community. Their constant presence is an important element of stability and maturity in the dynamic life of the oratory-youth centre. Among the adults, those who have specific functions of animation stand out, such as the parents and the family leaders. Likewise, in Salesian school environments, it is particularly incumbent on families to create this link with the educators-formators, to participate personally, through the school bodies, in the life of the school in terms of planning, educational reviews and taking part in school activities. In Salesian social work, the union and the consistent relationship with family members and with other institutions in the area or organisations that work in the same field are also essential.

In the same way, the auxiliary and administrative staff of a Salesian institution are also part of this network, contributing in particular to teaching and learning through the care of the environment, the social aspects and the effective logistical and organisational functioning. This means that they undertake their own work as an essential support for the organisation and contributing to the education of young people.

On the other hand, a Salesian institution or environment is meant to be a 'welcoming home', a living space for young people, a community-family in which the young people themselves are the protagonists of their education: a youth environment imbued with the values of the Preventive System, with well-defined spiritual and pastoral characteristics, with clear objectives and a combination of roles designed with young people in mind. It is important to remember that it is from this type of community of young people that the Salesian Congregation and the Salesian Family were born.

2. The greater involvement of the family, the first and indispensable educating community, is a challenge in this educational network; moreover, we recognise that the family is the nucleus of society and of the Church. For parents, education is an essential duty; they are directly responsible for the process of their children's growth, assuming the original and primary vocation of educating. This task is indispensable and inherent and therefore cannot be totally delegated or taken by others.

Without any doubt, families have their own particularities, given their history, the type of relationships that have been built, the intergenerational values and inevitably by the social, cultural and religious context in which they live. These realities influence the background and the way in which parents educate their children or understand their level of responsibility towards them and towards society itself. However, it is also true that all of these situations make their educational responsibility more and more complex. Let us explore, as an example, some phenomena that have a direct impact not only on the socialisation of children, but also on the way in which their ideas of the world and their relationship with it are being configured: the disintegration of the nuclear family, the multiple occupations of different members of the family unit, which affects the time and quality of coexistence, the lack of economic and educational opportunities, and the problems of intergenerational communication, among others.

For all these reasons, careful discernment is needed in order to recognise and respond to the most urgent or emerging problems of the family, making use of its many resources. It is interesting and promising to see the emergence of counselling centres run by both lay and consecrated people, with the aim of strengthening education and helping with family problems. Also interesting are the attempts to accompany groups of parents who are involved in the faith education of their children.

In short, every educational-pastoral community is committed to making parents aware of their educational responsibility in the face of changing circumstances and to accompany young couples in particular, actively involving them. As a result of this joint work, the ever more participative involvement of the family in the educational-pastoral project must be ensured.

1.3. A specific animation service: the animating core

As we have just seen, everybody is needed and mutually essential for a collaborative animation in the Salesian educational-pastoral model. If this is so, the Salesian animation of the educational-pastoral community requires some specific leadership interventions that ensure the organisation, coordination, pedagogical accompaniment, educational guidance with its objectives and contents, and the formation of the subjects. Encouraging everybody's participation is the task of a group whose aim is, first of all, to promote the involvement of the greatest possible number of its members; then, to take care of the quality and coordination of these, and finally, to pay particular attention to the educational-evangelising identity and capacity, thus ensuring the Salesian uniqueness of the model and of the institutions is maintained. These people, with their charismatic witness, constitute the 'animating core' of the educational-pastoral community.

The heart, although a small organ in relation to the rest of the body, is capable of delivering blood, and therefore life, to all parts of the body, but only if all the valves work in synergy to achieve this. Thus, the animating core is a group of people made up of Salesians and lay people who identify with the Salesian mission, educational system and spirituality, and who jointly undertake the mission of convening, motivating and involving all those who are interested in the Salesian work.

What is the role of consecrated persons in this context? The oratory-youth centre and the school are aimed not only at the young people, but also to the Salesian religious: protagonists and, at the same time, recipients of the pastoral offer. For this reason, all the religious, and not only those in charge, have a specific function of animation. This means establishing with the young people the same relationship that Don Bosco had, taking care of the witness of fraternal communion and of a cordial animating presence. The religious community also offers experiences of faith and prayer shared with them, as well as initiatives to engage in ongoing processes of formation in which consecrated persons are the first to be called to active participation.

In the structures for welcoming university students, the director and the Salesian community are responsible for the direction and animation of the university institution, as well as for the structure for welcoming university students. Normally, there is a nominated responsible person, Salesian or lay, who, in the name of the community, ensures the guidance and management of the college or residence and the development of the formative programme.

The religious community is part of the animating core of the Salesian parish and assumes a unique role in it: it is a witness to the primacy of God; it visibly manifests its fraternal life and the practice of the evangelical counsels, with its moments of prayer, of meeting, of relaxation, and shares this witness with the laity of the parish community. The consecrated person participates in the life of the parish, taking an interest in the history of the people, especially the young. The religious community creates around the parish priest a team of animators of the parish ministry and promotes the development and realisation of the pastoral plan; in collaboration with the parish priest and his team, it is responsible for the formation and spiritual animation of the faithfuland guides the members of the Salesian family so that they may be the first collaborators in the development of the project.

In social work, the primacy and coherence of the Salesians' rigorous witness makes their solidarity and educational presence among young people fruitful: they accompany them, sustained by a deep faith in God the Father, who wants all to "have life and have it abundantly" (Jn 10:10), while they acquire an ever deeper knowledge of the surrounding social reality and its mechanisms.

1.4. The educational-pastoral community, a significant experience of the Church rooted in the area

A Salesian educational-pastoral community has good reasons to participate actively in the social sector. Embedded in the community, the Salesian educational-pastoral model can unfold an extraordinary educational potential. The Salesian mission collaborates with and is open to all those who work for the promotion and formation of young people in specific cultures, to former students—boys and girls—who feel in solidarity with it, to the young people and adults of the area, to whom it offers its educational approach. Without claiming to be exhaustive, we consider it useful to recall these four aspects which affect every educational-pastoral community:

• First, it is integrated into the educational and evangelising movement of the local Church, introducing the Salesian formative approach in the area, coordinating its work with the other Christian forces that work for the education of young people.

• Secondly, it acts as a common meeting place with the social agents in the area that work for similar goals. It tends to integrate itself in this environment in which it lives, maintaining a dialogue and an enriching interaction; it participates in the formation and social and Christian promotion of all young people; it radiates sensitivity and co-responsibility towards those on the margins of society.

• It also acts as an agent of environmental transformation, encouraging conversion of situations that are contrary to Gospel values. It helps to discern the signs of God's saving presence. It is present in disadvantaged settings, paying attention to the elements that most influence their education and evangelisation. It participates decisively in the cultural debate and in the educational processes through various forms of association, voluntary and social cooperation, and cultural evangelisation. It brings an original educational proposal for the creation of a social and a civil conscience, in Christian solidarity.

- With criteria based on coexistence, it acts as the presence of the Church in multireligious and multicultural contexts: with this in mind, it must always be open to dialogue and collaboration with the various religious traditions, promoting with them the holistic development of the person and his or her openness to transcendence.

2. A Home Tailored to the Most Vulnerable and At-risk Young People

What permeates and unifies the inexhaustible and multifaceted activity of Don Bosco is the preference, neither exclusive nor excluding, for the poorest, the illiterate and the orphans, for those who experience and suffer the effects of poverty, social exclusion, abandonment and marginalisation. Every educational-pastoral community builds its programme for the most vulnerable and at risk, to help them to accept the richness of life and its values and to prepare them to live with dignity.

The other relevant issue is that the general education aspect of the Salesian model considers all forms of poverty, old and new, beyond their mere economic significance, which is traditionally referred to as 'poverty'. The term 'new' seems to be aimed at establishing a classification according to a time criterion. This is not the case. Poverty is not only a material scourge; it also includes other broader meanings that are as old as time: limited access to education, culture, a home, work; the lack of recognition and achievement of human dignity; the prevention of exercising true citizenship. This situation is compounded for different reasons, by the experience of a fragile, emotional and fluctuating levels of freedom.

On this point, the Salesians are involved in various different sectors: educational institutions of all kinds, especially shelter and humanitarian intervention services for street children, child soldiers, children who are exploited and exposed to sex tourism, prisoners, refugees, orphans, the sick, drug addicts. Salesian prevention is expressed in a multitude of practical options, responding to emergencies with the operational diversity required by each context.

1. Don Bosco's decisive choice was always that of creating an educational community in which a series of initiatives would be adapted to the needs and progress of the poorest boys. His life journey contained those elements that characterise the essence of every vocation of an educator and priest: even as a young person, Don Bosco resolutely directed his dreams and his time towards pre-adolescents and adolescents; vocationally, he focused his life towards at-risk young people between 12 and 18 years of age;[2] in his house lived boys from the streets of Turin, students in need of hospitality, apprentices looking for a job and in need of initiation into the rudiments of working life. In that pre-industrial society, its streets, its squares, its workplaces, he created a place of initial encounter.

> I was horrified to see a crowd of boys from twelve to eighteen years of age; to see them there, healthy, robust and with alert wits, but idle, pecked by insects and lacking in spiritual and material nourishment.[3]

He developed the educational approach based on the idea that only when education takes place in a healthy space (family) is it possible to change, even if only in small steps, the lives of these children.[4]

As a practical educator and as a man of God, Don Bosco did not target only to small, privileged groups, but turned his gaze to the masses of young people. He welcomed them without exclusion or prejudice, recognising and valuing all that they had in their hearts (their dreams, their weariness of life and their challenges). Don Bosco was convinced that all young people are in some way potentially 'abandoned' and 'insecure'. Evidently this is an age group that had not reached adulthood, had not matured in character, was at the mercy of

---

2   This age was the official opinion of Don Bosco, in his full maturity, having given life to educational and pastoral, youth and community institutions. This is what we read in the text that Don Bosco himself wrote in the 'Constitutions of the Salesians', approved in 1874.

3   *MO*, 11.

4   Those boys were the cruel consequence of the Industrial Revolution that was changing Europe, a progress for which the price was being paid by the lower classes. Think, for example, that in ten years (1838–1848) Turin saw its population increase by 17% (from 117,072 inhabitants to 136,849). No more than 10% of this population spoke and understood the Italian language correctly; young people between ten and twenty years of age made up almost 20% (22,456), an ever-increasing number over the years, especially because they were useful as cheap labour.

many dangers and often lacking consideration in civil society. Many factors—chronological, psychological, cultural and social—converged in their turbulent self-realisation. Young people, already scarred by challenging conditions, lived in precarious situations, not only from an economic point of view, but also from a sociocultural, affective, moral, spiritual and religious perspective.

From his pastoral and educational perspective, Don Bosco himself chose the evangelical position of becoming poor with the poor, he forgot himself and his own comforts, he assumed a life dedicated to others so as not to lose anyone and to seek out those who were on the margins of society. Both the enormous educational and social work were complemented and sustained by a personal way of life marked by simplicity, poverty and ethical integrity, without abandoning his spiritual life and his cultural preparation.

He broke the traditional scenario; he changed the paradigm. This is a point of special interest in our study that characterises the Salesian educational-pastoral model. The experience of living a precarious and fragile existence with young people challenges every educational-pastoral community to personal and institutional conversion.

2. Deprivation and the faces of suffering, of fragility and of educational vulnerability affect the life of the whole educational-pastoral community. A young person with fewer possibilities is not fully themselves, they do not realise their full potential, they repress and waste their energies, they feel frustrated and doomed to failure. At the root is not having a choice, of not having control over one's own life; of being 'expropriated', in the most radical sense of the word.

Unfortunately, poverty is not eliminated but is changed and transformed; it is dynamic, it manifests itself in different forms and ways, but in the end, it always indicates the same reality. The accumulation of this poverty, which is common in developing countries as well as in the large cities of the most developed countries, paints a picture of the vulnerability of young people that urgently calls for a liberating educational intervention that compensates for personal and social inequalities.

Faced with serious situations of injustice and violations of human rights in our societies, the charism of Don Bosco and his educational system impels us to commitment, both personally and collectively. An educational-pastoral community is not indifferent to the harmful poverty of its members, it fights it and tries to prevent it with the power of education. In the face of a social reality that is so multifaceted, prevention must transform, through education, the structures of poverty and marginalisation, particularly of young people. With renewed courage, we have the possibility of offering preventive action that promotes good, educational interventions that reinforce all fundamental civil, cultural, religious, economic, political and social rights. Therefore, and in keeping with all the above, the consequences of the exclusion of some people and stories are so many and, above all, so strong that they encourage every educational-pastoral community to be practical and immediate, to be competent and passionate, to be committed and generous, to be spiritual and hopeful. This means becoming poor with the poor.

3. New Youth, Old Educators?

The organisational culture of an institution is an educational model that encompasses the set of experiences, habits, customs, values and beliefs that characterise it. This culture can be seen not only in the structural and organisational aspects, but also in the mood and style of the educators. This is why not just any type of educator will do. It is worthwhile now to reflect on each individual and establish the appropriate profiles.

Don Bosco taught through his many undertakings that you cannot be a good evangeliser if you are not a good teacher, someone who is in a constant process of vocation and mission. According to Buechner, vocation is the place where "your deep gladness and the world's deep hunger meet."[5]

We point briefly to the heart of the Salesian educator, who must equip themself with adequate preparation in view of the full realisation of the Salesian educational-pastoral model. In the process of its practical application, we will address the issue of his or her identity as a person, as a professional, as a Christian and as part of a formative model.

---

5   F. Buechner, *Wishful Thinking: A Seeker's ABC: A Theological ABC*, (London: Bravo Ltd., 1993), 119.

3.1. The holistic development of the educator as a person

—**Making education a vocational option, a life choice.** Being an educator encompasses all imaginable nuances, from a dull and frustrated life to a heightened sense of educational vocation. For us, the educator is first and foremost a human being, a historical subject capable of analysing their daily present, recreating their roots and mapping a future. As we have seen, Don Bosco gradually matured his educational vocation and his specific way of being a citizen, a Christian and a priest by making education a vehicle and a life choice. Today, as in the past, the Preventive System needs people who make education an element of personal unity, an inspiring and dynamic entity. A clear example of what is proposed in these lines can be seen in the reading of one of the chronicles of the Oratory. Here we find a beautiful expression that conveys a kind of inner enthusiasm, of abundant energy that encourages those who read it to understand what the deepest gladness and the deepest need of the world is—to rephrase Buechner—for Don Bosco:

> I am everything for you, day and night, morning and evening, at any time. I have no other aim than to seek your mental, intellectual and physical benefit. For you I study, for you I work, for you I live, and for you I am ready to give my life.[6]

This means that, in offering and continually deepening the theoretical and practical frame of reference of the Preventive System, the Salesian heritage demands competencies strongly rooted in inner motivations: to dedicate one's time, one's energies, one's knowledge and qualities in favour of the young; it is rooted in this capacity for perseverance, despite difficulties and disappointments. Today the Salesian educational-pastoral model cannot be lived in any other way, nor can it be entrusted to people who are without courage and who are permanently dissatisfied and pessimistic. Passion and a vocation for education are at the forefront of the educator's character.

Within this reconceptualisation of the teaching vocation, an original factor must not be forgotten. The first question that all educators must ask

---

6   R. Domenico, 'Cronache dell'Oratorio di S. Francesco di Sales', in *Archivio Salesiano Centrale* (Roma), issue 5 (1864), 10. For an updated understanding of the expression "I study for you" we refer to J. Vecchi, 'I study for you', in *ACG* 361 (1997), c. 14.

themselves is not: "What can I do for young people", but rather "Who am I?" This suggestion has often been attributed to Romano Guardini,[7] university professor and a great educator of youth.

Perhaps this is both the turning point and the starting point. It is necessary to understand and discover the readiness of the educator for the development of their own personal maturity. Committing to personal growth is not only about the cultural dimension, but also about others that touch the affective, relational or spiritual life. It is therefore necessary to cultivate personal balance, awareness and assumption of one's own capacities and limitations. Likewise, the development of emotional intelligence, which has to do with communication skills and interpersonal relationships.

The management of relational dynamics, so important in the interactions required by the Preventive System, can condition, in a constructive or negative way, the formation of the young peoples' personalities. Ultimately, 'educational love' is not just a relationship, but becomes an attitude towards life.

In short, everything is important, everything has an impact: experience and passion, integrity of values and the ability to communicate them. Everything can potentially help or hinder the formative work in the service of children and young people.

By way of example, in the Salesian oratory-youth centre, the young animators, identified with the Salesian style and charism, take on the educational mission of this environment and actively animate its implementation. Each group animator (sports coaches, art workshop leaders, etc.) is an educator who walks with the young people, who discovers with them, who allows himself to be questioned by them and who knows how to suggest new goals for personal growth with enthusiasm and determination: they have experienced the educational process that they animate, responding to a vocation and a life project that makes them grow as a person. They are also aware that, both inside and outside the oratory-youth centre, they are an animator, and therefore an educator, who lives the values that they advocate.

---

7   Servant of God Romano Guardini (1885–1968), Italian-born German Catholic priest, author and academic. He was one of the most important figures in Catholic intellectual life in the twentieth century.

In essence, educating in the twenty-first century is a complex human activity that requires multiple skills and, above all, keeping things in balance. Everyone has own personal style, which is important to know, in order to see which elements need to be counterbalanced. Consequently, all this information refers to the humanity of the educator.

—**A patient effort of adaptation and training**. The importance of lifelong learning has been emphasised from both within and outside the education sector. Education is no longer confined to a specific period of time, but has become a constant need throughout life, as the UNESCO Delors Report warned in 1996.[8] All kinds of reasons support this need. In our case, the educator is a mediator who is asked to make a patient effort of adaptation and reflective practice under various conditions.

1. The Salesian educational-pastoral model is not aimed at producing material goods, but to transmit and accompany aspirations, to form new people for today's world. The 'Salesian legacy', received from the various generations of educators, needs our own contribution to enrich it. We imagine education as the ascent of a mountain rather than as a flat path. It is a climbing adventure with steps, anchors and bridges. It is necessary to feel every stone, every part of the landscape, and to control the times, distances, unforeseen events. The educator is a continuous explorer.

Educating is an intersection of the intentions of both educators and learners. It is absolutely necessary to equip oneself with diagnostic tools, processes of reflection and self-evaluation that contribute to refining educational intentions, perspectives, objectives and practices. The great temptation for educators is to fall into professional obsolescence, to be content with what has always been done, to be reduced to 'copy and paste'.

Fortunately, every time we evaluate our personal contribution with our mission and our educational vocation, the awareness that we have to become more educated, that we need new cultural, pedagogical and pastoral competencies is reaffirmed in us. It is evident that the pedagogical work of the Salesian educator is not based only on the mastery of scientific or academic disciplines; it is born of a reflective educational vocation, capable of creating environments, of

---

8   International Commission on Education for the Twenty-first Century, *Learning: the treasure within*, (London: HMSO, 1996).

spreading and encouraging processes, of promoting a culture open to Gospel values and to the questions of faith that we ask ourselves.

If the future of the Salesian educational-pastoral method depends fundamentally on the educators who give it life, formation will then be an indispensable tool for its survival. Understood in this way, formation is not achieved only with conferences, studies and courses; formation is the readiness of the mind and heart to be educated in and through life. In a word, formation is aimed at a multifaceted personal conversion, it helps personal positioning and commitment. This availability is not improvised or appears out of the blue: it arises from a person who is intelligent, attentive and ready to learn.

In this sense, it is an invitation to venture into the unexplored, to become personally aware of where I am now, to feel strongly about what I want to change, to reflect on what my own inner core is and what the basis is of my deepest motivations.

The vocation to educational service requires moments of personal sanctuary to question oneself and let oneself be questioned about one's own convictions, to reflect inwardly about one's own motivations and expectations: knowing oneself removes fear and strengthens one's own identity.

2. Moreover, education cannot be seen only as a duty to adapt, an equally important obligation for all, a commitment centred on needs and on compensating for one's own shortcomings; one must think of personalised training as the core of a vocationally motivated person. It is an indisputable fact that the success of appropriate education begins well provided, well sought after and well-motivated. Formation does not begin well when it is imposed. Providing training is much more than just intellectually satisfying the trainer; it is essential to provide inspiration, to adapt experiences, to recommend training schedules, to provide ongoing training with ad hoc initiatives.

It is therefore necessary to consider that training programmes limited to specific knowledge or to the acquisition of skills and techniques, which may be professionally valuable, have proved to be insufficient. We are increasingly convinced of the importance of the educator involving themselves in ethical, relational, attitudinal and emotional aspects. One can possess all knowledge, master up-to-date teaching methods, display resources and professionalism;

however, the fruit of a Salesian educator's professional training is ultimately the result of their own personal training, which makes them a model to be identified with.

3.2. The professional competence of the educator

—**Favouring the processes of personalisation and growth**. The Salesian educator is aware of what is required to educate young people today. It is very difficult to take a 'group photo' of new cohorts, to develop a unified understanding of young people's world and their common identity. In advanced societies, moreover, the lines between the different stages of the lifecycle are becoming increasingly blurred.

1. We must always resist any form of indiscriminate generalisation and reflection that leads us to think of young people as a homogeneous and an amorphous presence. Rather than giving a definition, the educator can try to offer a description of some aspects.

• On the one hand, they distinguish the emerging values that attract young people: peace, freedom, justice, friendship, participation, the promotion of women, solidarity, development, ecological urgencies, the variety of cultures, peaceful coexistence between different people, commitment against any kind of abuse and against new forms of slavery.

• On the other hand, they perceive the growing difficulty in identifying a common sense of life; the prominence of the absolute importance of emotions and early experiences; the scattering of multiple worldviews, religious beliefs and anthropological models, sometimes the polar opposite of holistic education; the overvaluation of one's own goals and the devalued perception of the self (low self-esteem); individualism combined with multiple loyalties; the reversibility of decisions and the search for satisfactory levels of stimulation and excitement.

It is clear that these characteristics mark a very narrow perimeter for an adequate view of the condition of young people. What we are interested in underlining here is that the experiences lived by Don Bosco also led him to speak many times of the frivolity and instability of young people, of their lack of tenacity in carrying out their commitments and, consequently, of the need for preventive educational action. But, above all, he feels that in every educational space, formal or informal, the educator must seek and find the accessible place for the good of each individual. This is the profound conviction that every young person, however wounded, has a free space worthy of trust and appreciation.

This is where the focus needs to be: every educator must be attentive to that corner of light in order to stimulate, grow and help to give it structure. We must try to change our perspective. Yes, there is a point that, if addressed in a timely manner, triggers processes of improvement and awakens a desire for change. This educational optimism is one of the main success factors of the Salesian model. The educator has confidence in the young person without having naive illusions about his or her condition; the educator accentuates the point of goodness, even in the most needy, and tries to develop it through positive experiences of goodness. It is a meeting with the young people wherever they are, valuing and nurturing the natural and supernatural resources that each one carries with them.

2. The noun 'personalisation' and the adjective 'personalised' are part of the educational grammar of the Salesian educator. For this reason, their function is not so much to 'transmit' an ordered series of norms and principles as to 'extract' (*educere*) or, better, to awaken the incalculable potentials of each young person and make them flourish. In reality, it is a matter of believing in the transforming capacity of education, and for this reason the educator is required to have skills related to listening, to mutual respect in interpersonal dialogue and to the clarification of motivations. When we say that he or she is a 'teacher', we allude to the art of teaching, of becoming a teacher, of speaking from the heart, of communicating with life. He or she also accepts a positive attitude towards people and their changing situations, taking on challenges with calmness and optimism.

3. Finally, good educational leadership is required; that is, knowing how to motivate incentives and contacts, both vertical and lateral links, and interventions aimed at achieving important objectives. It involves always concerting efforts, encouraging expression, instilling optimism and hope, but also correcting deviations and pointing out the right paths. The educator-leader has a bold vision; in other words, they are capable of seeing things differently from other people, to imagine and create the future, to express it clearly to young people and to give them a personal role in achieving it:

anticipating the historical momentum of our times to offer today what will be best for tomorrow.

Thus, we call for a special intrapersonal intelligence (that which allows us to understand ourselves and others) and interpersonal intelligence (that which has to do with the ability to understand other people and work with them). Depersonalisation and the deterioration of communication in educational environments feed the painful process of estrangement, oppression and alienation.

We refer to 'servant leadership' that encourages people to pursue new goals, supported by the democratic participation of the community; 'moral leadership' based on permanent values related to identity; and 'transformational leadership', which favours, motivates and inspires positive changes in behaviour.

—**Educationally interpreting the current condition of young people.** From Don Bosco's first Oratory in the Valdocco area of Turin up to 1877, when he wrote his Preventive System, there is a long period of more than thirty years; and from this (1877) to 1884, date of the famous 'Letter from Rome', there is another considerable period of seven years. A long time had passed between one milestone and the other. This speaks of how Don Bosco, with the passing of time, continued to experiment, to innovate, to create his vision, together with his closest collaborators. Much more time has passed for us since Don Bosco's death in 1888. This makes us think how important it is to know one's own historical reference points, the essential exercise of getting closer to the reality we find ourselves in, to understand the new developments in order to translate them into the educational terms and practices of our time.

As with Don Bosco, a hermeneutic, i.e., a reasoned interpretation of the data in itself and in its context, is necessary if we are to operate effectively and correctly in reality.

One of the most innovative suggestions of the Salesian model is the cultivation of a critical intelligence, the ability to interpret the world in which we live; in other words, a keen awareness of the educational and pastoral urgency of each historical period.

The need to read the current condition of young people in an educational way requires us to be there and not outside the area where education is at stake. In the service of the 'app generation', we educators are also called to value the new spaces for the creation of links between young people. The rapid development of information and communication technologies has created unusual ways of sharing personal information that influences the sense of belonging and the way of approaching others (as we will see in Chapter Six). The educator must enter into a reality that involves diverse devices and experiences, new spaces, such as social networks. Educators need to understand the changes that are taking place, as well as the functioning of media and cultural enterprises.

Training in the critical and educational use of these tools is important for the individual to strengthen the capacity for self-regulation, the safe and effective use of the digital world, the sense of limit and respect, the civic sense and the appropriateness of relationships. By this we mean that educating requires a good dose of realism, i.e., lowering ideal judgements; if it is true that the learner has all the resources to realise their life to the full, it is equally true that, left to themselves, they could run the risk of not putting into practice or not fully realising all their possibilities for growth. From an educational point of view, this aspect of Salesian realism is extremely important. After a few forays into the reality of education, every educator discovers the importance of having one's feet on the ground.

3.3. The Christian dimension of the educator

—**Entering more deeply into the Gospel.** While recognising that this is not an easy question, especially in increasingly secularised, multicultural and multireligious societies, the identity of the Salesian educational-pastoral model does requires the educator to appreciate the meaning and the demands of an indispensable 'apostolic interiority'.

We can state without hesitation that only a 'person of interiority', i.e., one who is willing to cultivate one's own depths, has the capacity to listen, can distinguish between what is apparent and what is authentic, can be open to the needs of others and be affected by them. Identities are built only from interiority, and this reaches its culmination in the spiritual person who lives and walks in the presence of God, who has discovered God manifested in everyday history and, in particular, in the history of the young people in whose service they work.

There is ample evidence that the most deeply motivated people associate their desires and goals to a cause that is greater and more important than themselves. For this reason, the Salesian educator who finds their motivation in Christ, the Good Shepherd, lives an authentic experience of faith in their daily activity, which leads them to address life, reality and history from the perspective of the Gospel.

To make a stronger impact, it is not enough to be greater in number or to have more powerful means at our disposal; above all, we need to go deeper into the Gospel. The Salesian educator is a witness to the Gospel in the world of culture and education; or rather, a person who makes the Christian message relevant through their intellect, their heart and their works. We have tried to show elsewhere (Chapter Three) that the force of attraction which enlivens educational and pastoral action comes from pastoral charity, that is, from a vocational motivation of service to the Gospel. This basic option so permeates the conscience of the educator that all their activities, whatever their nature, take on an evangelical intentionality (cf. Ezek 34:11, 23: the true shepherd).

It could be that the educator involved in formation work is not aware of this interiority or has not stopped to think about it. However, the reasons mentioned above allow us to affirm that truly competent formators, who unify in their lives a Gospel interiority and a rich humanity, are much better able to face the complexity of the education of the new generations.

Paternity, that of God and that of humankind, is defined when it engenders life under the banner of gratitude. We can say that generating life always implies a dying, which for educators is never to lose oneself, but always to find oneself in a fuller life. How much young people need not only to know themselves, but also to feel that they are being looked upon with kindness! We can affirm that they have the right to experience the fatherhood of God in the disposition of their educators. Their way of thinking, of speaking, of feeling, of behaving, makes God's benevolence transparent.

—Educators are, therefore, highly visible exemplars. Guided by this apostolic interiority, the evangeliser is aware that their message lies not only in the validity of what they proclaim, but above all in the conviction of the example with which they propose it. Education cannot be understood without a coherent way of life from the start. The educator has to go ahead in the effort to bring to the reality of their own life the values that they propose to the learner. We will have to imagine customs, styles, timetables, ways of life and structures that become as transparent as possible. Testimony creates added value for people, gains ground over discourse and reveals the purposes of what moves us.

As we said above, the Salesian educator is a visual and evocative metaphor with their attitudes and behaviour, with their good examples, not intended to be imitated, but to show the possibility of a life altered by the Gospel and thus to help each young person to make their personal interpretation. In other words, the Salesian educational-pastoral model needs not only teachers open to the enlightening power of the Gospel, but also transparent and suggestive witnesses who enlighten the eyes of the young. Those who add, who encourage, who accompany, who ask questions, who call, who excite, who preach by example, who provoke joy and good humour. In short: people with a great spirit.

Educational action is always a mediated exchange of words, gestures, looks, attitudes; the very presence of the educator is already educating, transmitting something that can be admired, enjoyed, imitated or denied. The witness is not a uniform, it is not a timetable; it is rather a committed life.

In this sense, it is necessary for every educator to consciously strengthen his or her motivations, so that service is born of a sincere desire for life and the promotion of life. The educational journey can alter the heart—in the biblical sense—of the person. A concept of Sacred Scripture, that of the heart, which reaches the innermost part of the person: yes, feelings, but also memories, images and ideas, interests and desires, ideals and values, i.e., everything that is experienced and needed to unify a person inwardly so that its outward manifestation is equally harmonious.

In the light of this reflection, we conclude by recalling that individual witness is incomplete today: the personal integrity of the educator is ensured and strengthened in an educational community and in an environment that makes this unitary vision of the approach discernible. The values that are lived, the behaviours that are manifested, the activities that are promoted, the signs and messages that are communicated, would be neutralised if the environment that the young people occupy was not consistent with the educational-pastoral programme.

3.4. The Salesian educational-pastoral experience of the educator

—The active presence of the educators among the young people. This picture of indicative characteristics is completed by a further element: the type of educational interaction and communication that is established between the educator and the young person. For this reason, educators must not delegate this personal relationship between young people and educators to others.

The Salesian educational relationship is an art that takes the form and colour of the wisdom of listening and communication. It is also often linked to questions of identity and belonging, i.e., our relationship with young people is possible if they associate us with some element of their daily life and if we frequent their gathering places. As a consequence, it is essential to make an effort to be where young people live and meet.

For example, educators in schools and vocational training centres not only teach in the classroom, but also work, live together, study, celebrate and pray together with the pupils: "Teachers in the classroom and brothers in the courtyard" (Don Bosco).

This requires the physical presence of the educator, proactive and liberating, with the style that Don Bosco called 'assistance' (which we will see in Chapter Six), intended as tailor-made accompaniment, animating closeness, attention to everything that happens, with the possibility of timely intervention and example. A very eloquent scene in the life of Don Bosco is represented in those improper attitudes of some priests of the time, formal but remote and distant in comparison with the paternal attitude of the priest Don Calosso:

> I knew some good priests who carried out their sacred ministry for the good of the people; but with none of them could I establish a family relationship. Often, I had the occasion to meet my parish priest in the street with the

curate. I would greet them from afar and, as I approached, I would also bow to them. But they would return my greeting in a grave and courteous manner and would go on their way without further ado. Many times, crying, I would say to myself and also to others: "If I were a priest, I would like to act differently; I would like to approach the children, to say good words to them, to give them good advice".[9]

It is an obligation to be open to each and every young person, without minimising educational expectations, but offering what is needed 'here and now'. This active decision implies welcoming young people at their current stage, so that they can gradually awaken their potential, unfold their resources and open their lives to new perspectives through a variety of educational and religious paths.

For this reason, we must pay attention to educators who suffer from 'emotional and relational illiteracy'; that kind of emotional and distant immunity towards young people.

—**Pastoral intelligence to energise pastoral planning**. The implementation of the educational-pastoral model needs to bring into play a great variety of factors: people, processes and activities. All this must be adequately geared to the objectives, contents and strategies of the pastoral plan to realise the Preventive System.

It is obvious that the Salesian—and Christian—vision of humanity calls for this kind of 'highway code' that gives indications on how to navigate the territory of young people. As we have argued above, the pastoral plan is not only and not primarily a directory of initiatives and allocation of resources, but it captures the kind of person we want to promote, calling for various essential personal attributes, without being disproportionate or unbalanced. It is a pedagogical instrument that expresses what we understand and how we shape the person we want to form. Therefore, it is not a closed formula, but an open one, with a capacity for flexibility and adaptability. It responds in this way to two great objectives—to humanise young people and to educate them to faith—by means of the four dimensions that integrate and enrich the fabric of the person (as we will see in Chapter Five).

---

9   *MO*, n.4.

With this approach, the Salesian educator has to provide some tools for improvement and change. On this point we refer to planning and evaluation:

• Today, a planning mindset is essential for effective and intelligent functioning in educational-pastoral settings. Without planning there is neither a careful analysis of reality (faithfulness to the young) nor a clear and shared definition of pastoral objectives (faithfulness to God). There is nothing worse than a short-sighted educator. We need people who are capable of taking other people by the hand (accompany), educators with ideas full of educational intent, appropriate and strategically planned interventions, necessary for the harmonious progress of an educational process. We know that any educational activity is effective when it is well planned and motivated.

• Evaluation processes urgently require the implementation of self-evaluation. To evaluate is not only to recognise the achievements and limitations of what is being evaluated, but also, to a large extent, to evaluate the personal attitude and the atmosphere in which the evaluation takes place. This continuous improvement invites us to work on personal and collective satisfaction with the objectives proposed in the pastoral plan. Consequently, all these improvement tools enable us to provide more appropriate responses to the needs of today's society, and from there to articulate the management and organisation of the institutions. They constitute a fantastic treasure trove that is extremely useful for any institution that is considering implementing a process of change.

These tools for improvement and change are not only of secondary importance, because a good project demonstrates the degree of success of the decisions taken, of the appropriate use of available resources and of the attention required to recreate them. Educating without planning is like constructing a building without structural plans or a design brief. It needs to stop and reflect; to analyse what has happened in order to assess and plan opportunities and identify solutions. That is programming: applying the best energies according to motivational priorities; knowing what to aim for, how fast to go and how to contribute one's input and rationale; managing distributions and also prioritising the search for new solutions. The final results reward this effort of thinking through and refining goals.

Perhaps one of the most important lessons is to not overlook the of dissemination what we are planning; a written project, expressing visions and options, makes it possible to inform about the suitability of the interventions and the resources put into play.

Another no less important consideration can be added to promote the co-responsibility, cooperation and coordination of everyone around a shared project of Christian humanism: teamwork. This method is based on the creation of cooperative forms of organisation, on respect for each person's responsibilities and decisions. As mentioned above, the leadership of an educational-pastoral model is exercised from a vision, an attractive and inspiring manifestation of what we want corporately. The vertical methods of organisation are giving way to new models of leadership, governance, work and decision-making that are more decentralised and collective, with a view to strengthening institutional identity and involvement. Although educators do some of their work individually, if the institution as a whole is to evolve, there must be many opportunities for the team of educators to learn and plan together.

Chapter Five

The Programme:
The Person We Aspire To Be

/@agustindelatorre.com

1. An Anthropology at the Heart of the Educational Experience

In a changing world such as ours, theological and anthropological reflection is intended to accompany the various educational models in their various contexts. The Salesian educational-pastoral model is not only action, praxis, organisation of resources and programming of interventions; it also involves a careful and intense anthropological, educational and theological reflection.

As the title of this chapter indicates, we are going to approach the programme of the Salesian educational-pastoral model from the perspective of the person that we intend to form. Much has been said about the 'art' and the 'science' of education, but what is certain is that in order to bring about the holistic development of a person (to educate), it is necessary to have a way of conceiving and interpreting the human being; therefore, it is necessary to ask oneself about the type of anthropology to which one must commit oneself in order to illuminate the educational task, or who we educate and what do we educate them for. In other words, to understand that every educational approach springs from an idea of mankind.

All educational practice, then, is embedded in an anthropology from which it becomes reasonable and understood. This choice does not exclude respect for the growth and characteristics of each person, nor for the life choices they may make in their lives.

Each anthropological model generates its correlative educational model. Furthermore, the Salesian educational model, as a paradigm that guides action in the work of each person involved in the formative process, must explicitly explain how the 'concern for' and the 'question about humankind' is understood. More specifically, it has to ask itself what concept of young people, in their multiple dimensions, it is called to develop. In this way, the educational practice of the Salesian school is also based on an anthropological vision; in this case, an intentionally humanistic-Christian worldview of the human being comes into play.

In fact, when we approach the whole range of issues that appeal to the complexity and balance of the young person, we necessarily touch on aspects relating to their physicality, emotions and feelings, intellect, capacity for relationships, spirituality, openness to transcendence and active engagement in the world. So, if we want to provide society with people who are capable of living their being to the full, in each of its fundamental areas, we must embrace an anthropological paradigm.

To better position the following pages, we believe it is appropriate to add an observation: if education is always related to a project of humanity and society, we believe that Jesus of Nazareth is our first role model. He is the face and word of God, but at the same time the fullest and most complete example of a human being. His life, words, gestures and actions inspire us with an ideal that can be embraced in freedom and that can significantly contribute to the integration of the whole person in a life plan. It is about an understanding of the human condition inspired by the Gospel and, from that, of all the forms of activity that are appropriate to it.

1.1. The Educational-Pastoral Project: the willingness to be proactive with young people

This understanding of the person in the richness of their being opens us to multiple facets that are inclined to growth and, therefore, to education. With this in mind, we are aware that to educate means to accompany 'from the outside' in order to reveal all that is good, beautiful and true in a person. In order to be able to give an anthropological response to this purpose and not confuse the means with the ends, it is essential to know what we want to achieve with our educational action, what is the anthropological, pedagogical and spiritual frame of reference in which the beginning and ending points of the person's project are set out: a map to guide the educational endeavour and service towards the weakest.

1. This process involves mapping it out in practice, not just devising it, i.e., translating it into an actual project. The Salesian educational-pastoral approach is not a declaration of principles, but rather the focal point towards which values converge and the model of the Preventive System develops. It is an instrument that harmoniously links the formative goals of a model according to the temperament of the person to be accompanied. By giving it this name, we are pointing out that it is an institutional element of essential reference that confirms the will to be proactive with young people.

The concept of a 'project' is traditionally present in educational work. The pastoral plan is an operative tool that effectively ensures, through its component parts, the development of the young person's full realisation.

It is therefore essential to understand the contribution of reflection and planning as important processes that can facilitate clarity and establish shared meanings. It is a development that has three steps: first cognitively, i.e., the ability to plan; then on paper, i.e., to visualise it, to set it out; and finally putting it into practice, with the possibility of evaluating it. Don Bosco himself felt in his time the need for order and organisation of pedagogical interventions.

> Having thus established my habitual residence in Valdocco, I was determined with all my heart to promote everything that would help to preserve the unity of spirit, discipline and administration... the organic foundations of the Oratory.[1]

The pastoral plan is directed towards the achievement of a dream, of a mission. As we have seen, the main focus point of the whole dynamism of the Salesian educational-pastoral model is the young person in all their dimensions (physical, intelligence, feelings, will), of their relationships (with themselves, with others, with the world and with God), in the double perspective of the individual and their role in history (promotion of community, dedication to the transformation of society). We cannot separate one dimension from the other; all this is done with an eye to the unity of their existential dynamism and their human and spiritual growth.

2. The pastoral plan directs and guides this educational process in which multiple interventions, resources and actions are gradually interwoven and articulated, with particular attention to the poorest and those with the greatest difficulties. The world of youth calls for a renewed effort and a historical responsibility for the younger generation. Beyond educational despondency, which today has become a new rising value, every process must be lived with constancy, continuity and the collaboration of various educational agents. In this regard, it is necessary for everyone to identify with a common course of intervention, a project capable of continuing the 'tradition' and, at the same time, of integrating what is new, and of incorporating the Salesian charism.

For this reason, it is essential to be rigorous not only in the formulation of the objectives, but also in the way of looking at reality and continuously interpreting it. The project's framework of values is presented with a real and specific cultural and social context of the people to whom it is addressed.

The Salesian educational-pastoral model that is translated into a project is not only attentive to the positive aspects, to the new values and to the

---

1   *MO*, n.6.

possibilities of improvement; it also considers that all forms of poverty block or even destroy the educational resources of the person and hinder the growth of young people. The educator, with project in hand, has been trained in mindfulness and invented new ways of intervening restoratively with the challenge of developing diverse ways forward.

3. Evangelising and educating with a project is the Salesian way of empowering young people, conceived as the process of awareness that makes people aware of their abilities and potential and the relationship between these and the world around them. In other words, being empowered means developing confidence in one's own capacities and potential, gaining control over one's own path. Each person lives insofar as they aspire and project, insofar as they hope; they carry in the depths of their consciousness the fundamental tendency to be more themselves, to be endlessly fulfilled. This freedom represents a horizon of meaning, an ideal for which it is worth striving and fighting.

The educator knows that the formation of successive generations should not be considered an easy reality, but rather a possibility whose scope requires the implementation of programmed, shared and verified educational processes, avoiding unrelated, scattered and repetitive actions. Pastoral planning is a matter of solid decisions and strategies, simple and interconnected steps.

1.2. It is a shared process rather than a script

Reflecting on the 'idea of a person' with Salesian creativity through the pastoral plan would seem to be something else to do, an abstract activity, a technique to be followed, a duty to be paid. However, the opposite is true: designing the navigational chart that indicates what kind of person we want to form is a process rather than an end result, a way of involving and unifying forces. Pastoral charity does not fail to encourage and animate a certain pedagogical intelligence in daily practice; that is, an organic variety of concrete proposals and a broad understanding of the reality of young people.

1. The drafting of a document would only be the tip of the iceberg of a much deeper and, at the same time, necessary phenomenon: every project requires those who prepare, animate and live it to have an operational alignment around clearly defined and measurable criteria and objectives. Ultimately, it

involves influencing the what for, the how and the who; in short, what is the purpose of the educational programme, what are the means and strategies for it to be experienced and internalised; and who is going to transmit it? It must involve all those in the educational-pastoral community in order to unite the different efforts towards a common goal.

Therefore, planning is also a process of identifying an educational-pastoral community. It means to plan together mechanisms of action focused on the future that the educational-pastoral community has chosen as its mission. Indeed, because it is a process of the mind and heart, it creates and strengthens the awareness of the common enterprise; at the same time, it deepens the educational-pastoral vocation, which must be shared and evaluated throughout.

2. To conclude for now, projecting not only avoids the dispersion of action, but also guides and continuously monitors the educational-pastoral action in order to always achieve a greater impact on the region. Today the pastoral plan can and must be thought of in terms of the environment of the Salesian work; all institutions, especially educational ones, enter into a wider system of relationships with which they are confronted and within which they interact. A training project with its own personality is a reflection of the coherence of the educational-pastoral community that manifests itself outside its walls, making itself visible as an agent of educational transformation.

The effectiveness of the Salesian educational-pastoral model is the result of the leadership of the educational-pastoral community that works locally and also in the context of an educational alliance that is open to contributions from the surrounding area. Aiming towards this coordination and networking implies a serious commitment to taking a step beyond the careful management of the activities carried out internally. It is a matter of stimulating and extending the communication and commitment capacity of one's own values with other educational, social and religious institutions that operate in the same area; opening up to the building of new relationships, establishing an effective dialogue with the most diverse stakeholders that have an impact on the lives of the children and young people.

2. The Educational and Pastoral Community as a Dynamic and Comprehensive Process

So, after considering where we want to go (the model of the person), we are going to address some fundamental areas in the accompaniment of young people in their complex process of growth. These fundamental anthropological aspects, mutually related and complementary, are called 'dimensions'.

Each of these areas of growth has specific objectives that make it unique, even though they are intimately connected. They are not organised in sequence but are knitted into the singular dynamism of a young person's development. They all form a unit, and each brings its own uniqueness to the whole; each receives from the others a direction and some original emphases. Consequently, they call upon and nourish each other in every intervention, in every institution, structure or service.

Each approaches the individual from a different perspective This is why none of the dimensions alone can offer a complete vision of the human being; otherwise, we would fall into a simple and reductionist perspective. One cannot be developed without explicit reference to the others. They can be understood as communicating entities, according to the logic of a system—not a collection of characteristics—where the originality of a person is forged.

At the basis of this approach there is a precise anthropological, educational and theological objective that envisions the growth of the person as a coming together of maturity and a Christian sense of life. The programme aims at their overall salvation by focusing on divine and human dynamics working together.

Thus, the unity and correlation of the different dimensions must be explicit in the objectives and strategies of the PEPS, with the certainty that each step and each intervention is embedded in a process of unified growth, answering the question: what kind of young people should be supported? Possibly, in the light of this question and this reflection, it can be concluded that the combination of the dimensions stems from a concept that respects the completeness of a person's growth.

In the following we present the organic synthesis of the four dimensions. This presentation finds its roots in the detailed description in the Constitutions: "Our educational-pastoral service".[2]

2.1. The dimension of education to the faith

The Salesian educational-pastoral model is not satisfied with only contributing to the development of the physical, interpersonal, emotional and intellectual dimensions; being faithful to the meaning and purpose of its source of inspiration, the Preventive System, the spiritual dimension is vital for achieving human fulfilment.

The first element that stands out in this point is the consideration that every young person carries written in his or her own heart the desire for God, the aspiration for a full life in the unifying perspective of faith. When we presented the trinomial 'reason, religion, loving kindness', we focused on the importance of the religious dimension, which permeates all the fundamental dimensions of the person, giving it unity and meaning. Now we will focus on the process of growth and accompaniment.

To begin this reflection, it is necessary to abandon the conception of 'religion' as morality or education to the faith as behavioural education. Without going into a pastorally detailed explanation, we should take into account two facets that refer especially to the faith education of young people: the **religious question** and **the personalisation of faith**.

1. With regard to the first of these arguments, we would like to recall that the fundamental human experiences of young people should never be underestimated: they are, in fact, a window open to faith, even if they do not in themselves awaken it. They enable a person to travel to their inner self, to the sanctuary of their being. The nature of finite experience is precisely what communicates our limits and poses a set of questions: the challenge of death, the contradictions and fragility of life, the tenacity of pain and suffering, the meaninglessness; in short, the meaning of the person and of life. They are like arrows that open their hearts to new questions, searches and longings.

---

2   C, nn. 31–39.

These questions also challenge young people and raise questions that cannot be answered by submission, self-satisfaction or avoidance. Sometimes these questions find a certain answer in human wisdom. But others, most of them, remain open. It is a matter, then, of giving meaning to the person beyond one's own history, of assuming an experience of transcendence, in other words, a 'calling'. This call is the **religious question**. We can affirm that young people are a generation with a spiritual sensibility.

The formation of the person that we suggest includes educating in this inner dimension, with the desire that, implicitly or explicitly, the educational-pastoral model facilitates the guidance of young people in their encounter with Jesus Christ and the transformation of their lives according to the Gospel. In this moment of invocation, even if it is not very lucid or expressly formulated, the offer of the Gospel can resonate as a coherent response to the questions that the person is asking. It is the moment to offer the message of salvation that comes to us through Jesus Christ. Evangelisation brings the Good News of Christ to all the layers of humanity in order to renew it from within.[3]

2. Similarly, in the Salesian educational-pastoral model, a close practical relationship is established between the formation of a mature personality and sanctification. Holiness, that is, a relationship with God lived consciously and practically, is the goal to which every person, and especially the Christian, is called. Within it, in the image of Christ, the incarnate-God, there is a continuity and fusion between human maturity and grace. This translates pedagogically into a definite path of personal growth that assumes all the resources, values and riches of the person, and unites them in a unitary project. To this end, it calls for a pedagogical and evangelising approach to accompanying young people.

Don Bosco's pedagogy has an enormous interest in the complete salvation of each young person, in the holiness of their lives. It thus becomes the final option on which the person achieves wholeness. The 'holy person' is one who knows, loves and serves God; in doing so, they know, love and serve others. But, at the same time, it is a spiritual life ordered with balance and moderation. Recall, for example, how Don Bosco obliges his pupil Dominic Savio not to impose on himself penances that harm his health.

---

3   Cf. Paul VI, Apostolic Exhortation *Evangelii Nuntiandi*, n. 18.

Don Bosco transmitted the passion for the salvation of the young lived in the constant commitment of a simple and essential spiritual life, adapted to the condition, age and culture of the young, united to the other educational and recreational activities of the Oratory. The journey of the religious question, as a force of motivation and essential direction, does not take place at the end of a preparatory stage, but is implicitly at the heart of the first encounter and, explicitly, of every education to the faith. Don Bosco did not distinguish between the first proclamation and catechesis, but when he met a young man, he immediately invited him on a journey of discovery of the interior Christian life.

3. This journey of maturing in faith today requires long periods of time and methods that are more in tune with initiation. For this reason, a great deal of individualised attention is necessary in order to awaken the acceptance and internalisation of faith. If religious faith is not integrated into the lives of young people, if it remains foreign and incomprehensible, it can be taken on board, but in the future, it is quickly abandoned.

For this reason, we have chosen the expression educating 'to the faith', because it indicates the journey towards a decision that permeates thoughts, concerns and attitudes. The questions that arise almost immediately from the preceding statements are: how can we foster an encounter between the hearts of young people and Christ? In contrast, the expression 'education in the faith', while very rich in meaning, aims rather at accompanying those who have already accepted the call.

From the above, personalising the approach means adapting to the situation and possibilities of the different subjects: to remain vigilant, attentive, and recognising the value of each process, because, while maintaining the same points of reference and substantially the same demands for all, each one has to make his or her own way. It is a matter of building faith on the personal experience of God, which affects and illuminates the whole person, and which, in turn, requires paths of accompaniment and respect for the undeniable mystery of His person.

2.2. The educational-cultural dimension

In general, when we speak of 'education', we mean the process of maturation that unleashes the creative potential of the person and develops all his or her resources. When we talk about 'culture', we can understand it in three ways: as a person's disposition to cultivate his or her abilities; as an inheritance of knowledge, goods, values and meanings specific to a human group or a particular historical time; as the possibility to recreate or interpret that heritage in a personal process of assimilation, re-elaboration and enrichment.

It is also interesting to reflect on the dual purpose that we assign to the educational-cultural dimension, since, on the one hand, it serves the integral promotion of the person in all his or her potential (healthy, balanced and supportive) and, on the other, the systematic, active and critical assimilation of culture.

1. Among the characteristics of this dimension are physical and psychomotor development, which is closely linked to play and sports activities, physical expression, habits related to the care and hygiene of the body, external presentation and tidiness.

Another important aspect refers to the intellectual and cognitive terrain, in order to think and assimilate ideas, meanings and the proposals of science, of culture and of history. A very Salesian element is also the sensitivity and aesthetic capacity to enjoy the beauty of art and of nature.[4] The aesthetic experience, whether it consists in creation, the exhibition of beautiful objects,

---

4   Ecology has a great educational potential, because it can educate to beauty. This is the thesis of the Salesian Heriberto Cabrera, professor at the Cardinal Jean Margeot Maurice Institute and at the University of Laval (Canada). It is a quarry under construction in which one can move, embracing the intercultural and interreligious aspect; it is a place to grow in partnership and, finally, it offers multiple teaching opportunities to transmit, in a different way, values and knowledge. He further states that the chapter on the Preventive System and ecology in Salesian pedagogy has not yet been written; but, as in the mind of Don Bosco, it cannot be a simple theory, but rather the result of a re-interpreted and systematised experience (cf. H. Cabrera, 'To go the way of the Dodo. Sistema Preventivo e ecologia', in *Con Don Bosco, educatori dei giovani del nostro tempo*, 362–390).

even in the contemplation of them, has a high pedagogical and ethical value, because it teaches people and develops their humanity.

As we know, aesthetics is closely related to ethics, since the origins of our culture, beauty and goodness have been the ideals towards which humanity must strive. No less important, therefore, is the formation of the moral conscience and the capacity for ethical discernment for motivated and responsible judgement. The search for truth and adherence to it is part of this aspect. We are talking about an area that has to do with the conditions of autonomy and responsibility, for example, in regard to one's own work and the proper use of goods and money. It is a matter, then, of the meaningful constructing and positioning of the person, both in what concerns the private or individual dimension of morality as well as in what pertains to the public and collective sphere.

This approach also emphasises the particularly important role given to affective-sexual and volitional maturation, which enables self-giving and encounter. It manifests itself through the good use of emotions and personal interests, the appreciation of others, the respectful treatment of the other sex, the realistic self-concept and an adequate and progressive education for love.

This list of aspects, without being exhaustive, offers us the possibility of specifying more specific objectives within our approach.

2. Secondly, we want the young person to act as a critical and active subject within his or her own culture. It should be noted that the mission of the educator is to introduce the young person to the cultural heritage handed down by previous generations, to offer tools to reread the culture of their predecessors and the foundations that sustain humanity and its symbolic value. We try, therefore, to help them to shape their way of life and the corresponding way of knowing, expressing themselves and acting in accordance with the peer group in which they live here and now, always preserving a critical attitude and a keen interest in the enhancement of the culture they have inherited.

In this sense, the always open and unfinished formation of these aspects is important for a critical understanding of reality. This means that this dimension cannot be reduced to an accumulation of past knowledge, passively received by the subject (the so-called 'banking model of education'[5]); it requires a work of interpretation and an attitude of reflective listening. If we take into account that 'critique' (crisis) is everything related to discernment, in order to be able to discern from one's own conscience, the adoption of a precise system of values is required.

The educational-cultural dimension is intimately related to the dimension of education to faith. Education is the place and the mediation for offering the good news of the Gospel, a message that is incarnated in a particular culture and requires gradual processes to be assumed, in harmony with the maturing capacity of each young person. The proposal of faith, on the other hand, is intertwined with the objectives of human maturity, because it is there that it makes sense to believe. The evangelising gaze, therefore, is full of educational attention; it is an exercise in educational wisdom.

2.3. The experience of associations

This third dimension, in which we want to encourage the maturing of the community-associative experience and the sense of belonging, is for the reader's consideration.

The Salesian educational-pastoral model has in the associative experience one of its most important pedagogical intuitions. Don Bosco valued youth associations as an educational presence capable of multiplying formative interventions. As a young man, he himself created the 'Society of Joy' during the period in which he attended the college of Chieri, planning group activities. The associations, the societies, the conferences, each one in its own way and with its own interests and objectives adopted by the members, emerged at the beginning of the Oratory, and in the 1860s and 1870s, they appeared in the boarding schools and colleges.

The Preventive System requires an intense and transparent environment of participation and friendly relationships, stimulated by the animating presence of the educators. At the same time, it promotes all the ways that build activity and associative life, as a tangible initiation to community, civic and ecclesial commitment. From this perspective, the dimension activates various demands

---

5   Cf. P. Friere, *Pedagogy of the Oppressed*, (New York: Herder and Herder, 1970).

that have to do with a broad outlook of solidarity towards the environment, with the capacity to plan life in terms of listening and commitment to a social culture. Educating is that impulse towards openness to other worlds. It contributes to the growth of coexistence with a human face.

In other words, it is a question of forming a critical and creative awareness in order to learn, to know, to inform oneself and to become involved in the problems of one's own community. This aspect has a practical outcome, i.e., participation in activities that promote change in civil and political society. Put another way, to imbue the political, economic and cultural dimension with the Gospel, and to influence them ethically.

This depiction is intended to wish young people the best for the future, ensuring them a greater awareness of their own role in society in a context of 'multi-dependence'. This means that being members of associations helps them to become part of a democratic social and political life, to inhabit spaces of public presence, according to the demands of citizen participation that is interested in the collective as opposed to individualism. It is a stimulus to the education of civic virtue proposed by Don Bosco's expression: "honest citizens".

Therefore, this civic participation is a learned ability; it is not the result of automatic or magical situations, but of sustained and intentional training. It is about teaching the ability to become personally involved in life, in events and in history. This concept requires thinking about educational issues from the perspective of the socio-political education of young people, so that they have the tools, information and awareness necessary to discern and assert their voice, their rights and demands, just as they are required to fulfil their duties.

The purpose of this approach is also to point out the remarkable insights this dimension brings to the sense of belonging. The group preserves people from isolation and, above all, from the anonymous crowd. Active group membership invites not only rewarding components; it leads to the sharing of common, dynamic, preferably affective goals, always in a culture of symbols, commitments, rituals and beliefs. Learning to live together is not only learning to live with others, but to share a common set of core values, to pursue a common goal and to help each other in its pursuit.

2.4. The vocational dimension

Vocation is always a project: each one of us is the project of what we can be, of what we should become. Every project involves a twofold task: the effort of understanding it, sometimes intuiting it; and the effort of executing it, of defining it in a definitive way. For this reason, the vocational dimension educates the 'vocational call', that voice or inner ally, and at the same time, as a consequence, the 'vocational decision'.

1. A life plan, whatever its direction, cannot be completed if it is not worked on. It is not educated or guided by occasional and sporadic acts. Vocational guidance is a path that is travelled gradually, step by step; a task that lasts a lifetime. This is why the 'vocational question' is at the heart of the anthropological perspective, which tells us about the person and what the direction, purpose and function of life are.

It is clearly the dimension of seeking, and it consists of very rich educational elements that tend to awaken and illuminate this project and accompany its realisation. It would be necessary to widen the focus even more and ask ourselves if, when accompanying a process of growth and maturity of the person themselves, it helps to acquire the progressive awareness of one's own vocation and, consequently, of the personal, free and motivated decisions that it requires.

This formation needs not only time and space, it is not only a process; it should also be understood as a propitious moment in which a person matures their important decisions, i.e., gives a shape and meaning to life. The vocational offer must be present throughout the whole process of education and evangelisation, but youth is an opportune time to create these better conditions. It is during these years that choices are made that will determine their life for a longer period of time.

Personalised assistance, i.e., personal accompaniment, is precisely one of the fundamental issues to be valued. Accompanying a person brings with it the idea of a journey, a path, a trajectory, a movement to and from, an effort, a horizon towards which to advance. The challenge is to not abandon young people in the task of discernment, but to encourage each one to reach deep within themselves, to allow them to discover their promised land, to help them

140

to find their most profound truth. This is why spiritual mentors, sensitive to the realities of the inner world of young people, are still very much needed.

2. The first three dimensions converge in vocation, the definitive objective of our educational-pastoral approach. The objective is to accompany each young person in the search for their own vocation, the place of their response to the offer of free and unconditional love that God has in store for them.

The ultimate goal of all guidance is development of the person, but not in isolation of their own world. The Salesian educational-pastoral model accompanies this discovery and the development of personal journey that allows for a commitment to transform the world according to God's plan. The 'vocation' begins with the call to life, continues with the call to faith and ends with various responses to life choices.

The general requirement of this vocational guidance involves one condition: a gradual approach. Despite all the possible contradictions and difficulties, all vocational accompaniment must be undertaken with consistency, which implies clear objectives, sustainability, fidelity to the situation of each young person, progressiveness, adapting the contents and experiences to the needs of each one, and without infringing on their freedom. Every vocation is a personal commitment, it appeals to one's own responsibility: no process can be forced either from within or from outside.

This requires rationality in the motivations, in the processes and in the incentives; only in this way does it lead to an individual's true capacity to listen and to respond to God. This gradual approach demands a broad perspective in presenting all vocations, from the most generic and common to the specific and diverse, according to each young person's path. For this reason, vocations animation finds its undeniable means of intervention in the accompaniment of the apostolic vocational option.

The four fundamental dimensions are summarised as follows:[6]

---

6   Cf. *Salesian Youth Ministry. Frame of Reference*, 149.

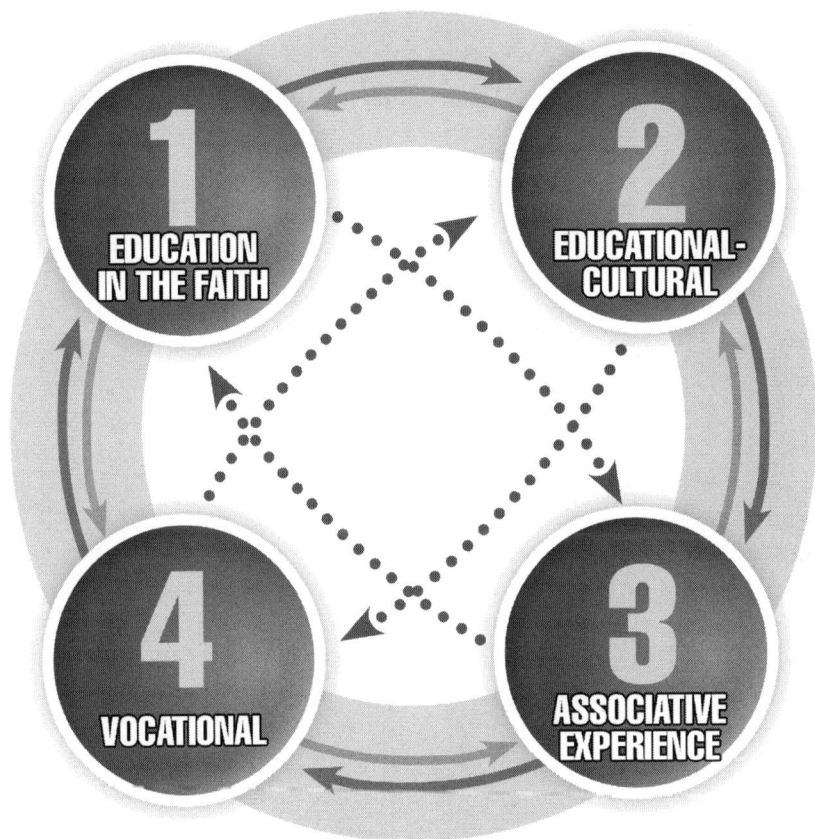

- **Education in the faith** [1] is not possible if it does not become an educational and cultural path [2] that includes the relational and associative dimension of the person [3], who can only then discover and direct his or her own life towards its fulfilment [4].

- The **educational journey** [2] cannot develop, i.e., lacks the anthropological truth of reference, if it is not aspired to the idea of humanity proposed by evangelisation [1]; moreover, it does not achieve its own objective if it does not involve the person, taking into account all of their relationships [3] and the objective of developing one's own life according to a robust and guiding plan [4].

- The **personal and associative relationships** in which we live [3] are merely a physical closeness if they are not incorporated in some way into a full personal and cultural maturity [2], if they are not considered in one's own life plan as indispensable for one's own personal growth [4] and if they do not find in evangelisation the very definition of loving relationships [1].

• The **vocational dimension** that guides our whole journey [4] is incomprehensible without the reference to Christ [1], if it does not affect the relationships that each one has in one's own life [3], and if it does not become the meaning and the goal of one's own cultural and educational formation [2].

To conclude, after having defined the meaning and substance of the educational and pastoral community, it is possible to think more broadly about the stages of its production. To this end, we refer to the second part of chapter 8 of the 'Salesian Youth Ministry Frame of Reference', which aims to offer operational guidelines and concrete models for the design of the educational and pastoral community. This chapter presents a reading of the various educational-pastoral tools that are flexible, simple and easily accessible to all, and how they are to be understood and applied within an organic approach and at different levels.

Chapter Six

The Salesian Style of
Our Educational Service

1. The Preventive System as a Pedagogical Criterion and Practice

We have focused on how the educational-pastoral community is a living organism that exists in the measure in which it grows and develops. For this reason, we should not only or even mainly pay attention to its organisation, but also to its way of life, its methods of animation and accompaniment of the people who constitute the community.

In the preceding pages, we have gradually explored the meaning and aims of the Salesian educational-pastoral model, as well as a snapshot of its origins in the characteristics and the path followed by Don Bosco. Based on its guiding and inspiring principle, the Preventive System, we have described the type of person and the dimensions to be developed and cared for in every educational-pastoral community.

Now, coming to this chapter, we turn our attention to the method, both conditioned and, at the same time, conditioning the educational environment offered by the charismatic (educational-pastoral) model we have described.

To understand the scope of the concept of 'charism', we must refer to the religious domain; however, it sometimes has effects in educational areas, because it influences the formation of an educational style. In fact, there is a link between the Salesian charism and the educational style that is formed through the care of relationships and the established climate: the former is the essence of the latter, and the latter its more tangible manifestation.

Let us recapitulate: Don Bosco, together with his collaborators and the first Salesians, had already embodied in the Oratory that particular experience of community. Moved by the Spirit—the charism—he had given shape to a particular style that defined the way and manner of carrying out his project. The Salesian work, begun as a 'simple catechesis' (1841), gradually expanded with a distinctive style that gave its own character to festive oratories, Sunday and evening schools, training workshops for the formation of young workers, schools, orphanages and boarding schools. For this reason, today we refer to the Oratory of Valdocco not as a historical or documented exercise of what happened then, nor as a nostalgic faithfulness that reproduces the past in the present; it is rather a way of returning to the origins in order to look ahead, a source that continues to inspire works and activities, a culture of relationships fitting to the reality of youth. When we approach the oratorian experience, the first thing we discover is precisely that: its durability and its capacity to travel through time to the present day.

The educational-pastoral model of Valdocco was and is conceived as a total and positive system of education; it is born for the group and for each individual, for every type of environment and educational context. It is established within a process that does not advance linearly, but in a spiral, and that integrates many methodological elements that we will analyse in this chapter.

From these and other similar considerations cited in this text it could be deduced that the 'Oratorian criterion' is the permanent indicator of the Salesian educational style, it provides the matrix of evaluation for Salesian educational-pastoral action. It is therefore the model that guarantees the consistency of all institutional interventions and activities, the fundamental norm for the discernment and renewal of every educational establishment. An excellent summary of this approach was written by Don Bosco's eighth successor, Fr John Vecchi:

> When we think of the origin of our Congregation and Family, from which Salesian expansion began, we find first of all **a** community, which was not only visible, but indeed quite unique, almost like a lantern in the darkness of night: Valdocco, the home of a novel community and a pastoral setting that was widely known, extensive and open... Such a community gave rise to a new culture, not in an academic sense but in that of a new style of relationship between youngsters and educators, between laity and priests, between artisans and students, a relationship which had its effect on the area and on the city itself... All this had as its root and *raison d'etre* the faith and pastoral charity, which tried to create from within a family spirit, and led to a deep affection for God and our Lady.[1]

Inspired by this 'oratorian criterion', the Salesian style was created, which is its most characteristic and expressive depiction. It is presented as a typically Salesian educational method of living together and in communion, which has a specific expression in evocative icons: 'house', 'parish', 'school' and 'playground'. These images, typical of the Salesian vocabulary, do not specify exact environments, spaces and places, but rather the **educational process** The diagram overleaf provides a clear representation of this Salesian style.

---

1   J.E. Vecchi, 'Now Is The Acceptable Time', in Direzione Generale Opere Don Bosco, *Acts of the General Council*, (Rome: Editrice SDB, 2000), 23.

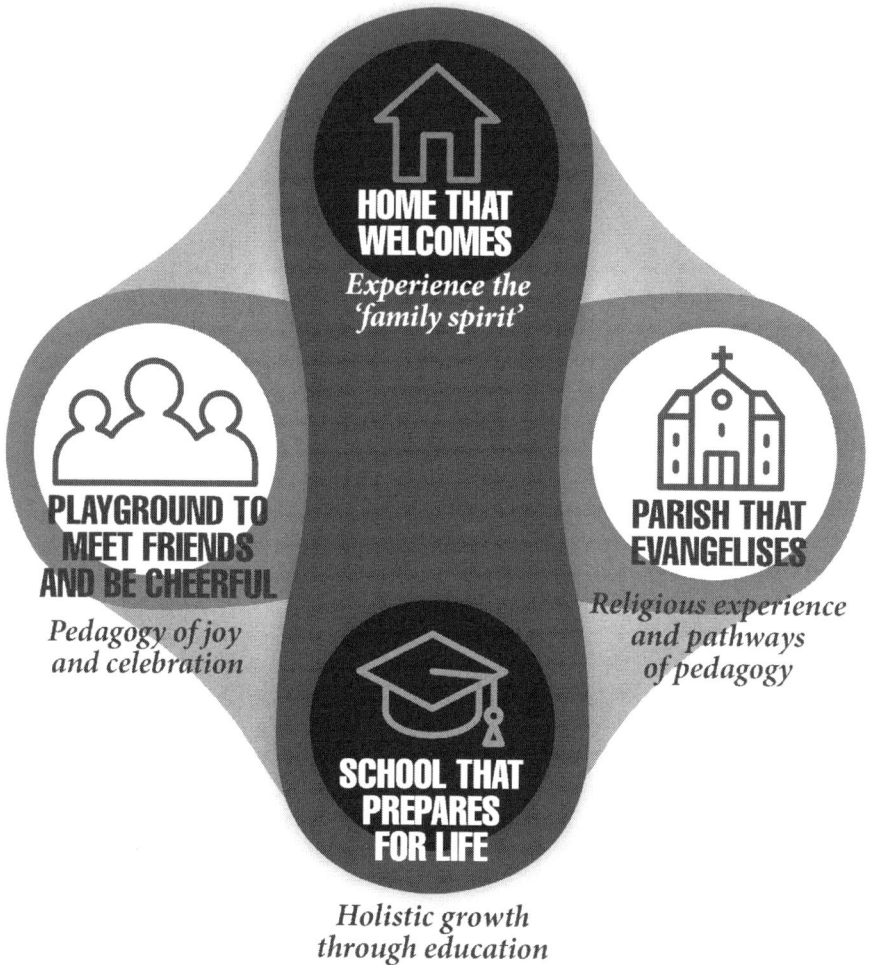

HOME THAT WELCOMES
Experience the 'family spirit'

PLAYGROUND TO MEET FRIENDS AND BE CHEERFUL
Pedagogy of joy and celebration

PARISH THAT EVANGELISES
Religious experience and pathways of pedagogy

SCHOOL THAT PREPARES FOR LIFE
Holistic growth through education

2. Living Together and in Communion in the 'Salesian Style'

The expressions of the Salesian educational-pastoral model resemble a kaleidoscope, through which the Preventive System is observed in its various aspects: it is practised in a family climate enriched by an educational and positive atmosphere ('home'), marked by joy ('playground'), where the young can acquire and develop all their potential and abilities ('school'), and walk following a clear path of faith ('parish').

The Salesian style tries to proportionally combine an environment with familiar, cultural and religious elements, a complete educational experience expressed in four images. These are the 'Salesian commandments' to which every educator must return, refer to, and measure him or herself against. They presuppose multiple and complementary practical expressions, and none of them should be neglected. Let us look at them through some examples.

2.1. A welcoming home (experience of a 'family spirit')

The Salesian educational-pastoral model needs to evaluate the degree of familiarity in each establishment; to sincerely examine the fulfilment of Salesian assistance and to resolutely choose personal accompaniment, trying to reach out to everyone in a distinctive way. As will be seen, the meaning of the 'welcoming home' needs to be rethought, reformulated and permanently reorganised in the educational-pastoral environments and services.

1. From the outset, this icon refers to an atmosphere rich in familiarity and trust. In using the term 'atmosphere' or 'climate', we have recourse to a metaphor borrowed from meteorology. Just as climates influence the behaviour and even the characteristics of living beings, so the 'atmosphere' of the Salesian house is the prerequisite that explains the behaviour, identity, values and relationships that people develop.

Don Bosco underlines that there are many nuances in considering the formative value of a positive educational environment. He knew this well, especially when he visited the prisons and walked the streets and squares of Turin. In the best Salesian educational tradition, this familiarity intersects with the elements of a healthy, familiar, welcoming, close, enriching and integrating environment that responds to the educational needs of young people, a 'home', as demonstrated by the experience of Valdocco. The environment is not a geographical issue but involves creating a favourable climate for formal and informal living.

The malaise of many young people alongside antisocial behaviour always has a cause, one of which is the relationship with the environment. The Salesian educational-pastoral model is, therefore, an authentic 'pedagogy of the environment' where all the elements contribute to a holistic approach to the emotional health of young people, overcoming all forms of generalisation, standardisation or discrimination. It is a matter of caring for this natural space where people live, their relationships, their cycles of interaction and the modelling of their personalities.

This educational ecology is born out of practice. An example of this can be seen in Don Bosco's time, when the house was decorated with large posters hanging on the walls with phrases in the same language and tone which Don Bosco used, and which recalled his words or reminded others of him when he was not present.

2. But, above all, there are two facets that build this ecosystem of relationships: the example set by adults and the capacity for welcoming people. In this setting, various adult figures can be identified on the one hand: attractive biographies in a climate where contacts and affection circulate. Each of these people makes his or her own contribution and leaves the impression of his or her personality and competence. Particularly in certain stages of personal development (adolescence), role models are needed in order to compare one's own life project and to stimulate its implementation.

The young people in an educational-pastoral community are sensitive and receptive to what is happening. For this reason, it is necessary to ensure diverse figures that promote relationships between the worlds of adults and young people; relationships that go beyond the purely functional to strengthen those that are exemplary, i.e., respectful, fraternal and caring.

On the other hand, it is necessary to make each child or young person feel at home, welcomed, unconditionally accepted, showing their originality and uniqueness. It is not only a stage in the socialisation process of a young person in a group, but an attitude of the educator to be there for young people and ensuring that they know it. To offer them a 'family' in the proper sense of the term, a listening ear that responds to their need to speak, to be heard and to be recognised.

Any young person entering a new environment inevitably feels a sense of insecurity. This perception will vary in intensity depending on the personality type and experiences in similar situations. In this circumstance, they need to be reassured that there is someone available to turn to, that they are being cared for personally and directly. The path from being welcomed to having a sense of belonging (feeling accepted and involved) is not a long one. In fact, for young people, their identification with the circle of people to whom they belong and with the *modus operandi* of the environment in which they live is undeniable. They feel happy and integrated not only in active participation, but also in the emotional sense, thanks to which they feel connected to the group by reciprocal bonds of friendship and by adhering to its values and customs.

It is important to organise welcoming activities and to establish the most attentive accompaniment at these times. It is a kind of collaborative care in which each of the personal stories can be expressed, nurtured and guided. The impact of those who arrive for the first time in the Salesian house and see that their needs are respected and responded to is positive. However, this dimension must be active and available in the future to promptly detect and respond to critical moments or circumstances of a personal nature that may arise.

3. Moving on to another consideration, we maintain that in order to gain moral authority in the world of young people, it is necessary to cultivate trust, an indispensable condition for the success of education. It is a matter of exercising a type of authority that inspires respect, trust and affection.[2] This cordiality guarantees the effectiveness of the norms of an educational environment and asserts the positive acceptance of adult guidance and encouragement. The formula *plus amari quam temeri* (to be loved rather than feared) was a fundamental principle of Don Bosco. Although it is not original to him,[3] it had a special echo in Don Bosco's words: "Act in such a way that all those with whom you speak become your friends."[4]

---

2 The Salesian Jean-Marie Petitclerc, director of the Institute of Vocational Training 'Valdocco' (France), speaking of the relevance of the Preventive System in a changing society, affirms the need to establish authority over the quality of the educator/young person relationship characterised by trust (cf. J.-M. Petitclerc, 'Il Sistema Preventivo ripensato nell'orizzonte attuale', in Orlando [ed.], *Con Don Bosco, educatori dei giovani del nostro tempo*, 77–87).

3 It is difficult to establish an exact chronology showing the history of the development of this expression. It certainly formed part of the monastic life of St Augustine and St Benedict, as well as in some medieval authors of humanist pedagogy and in the Renaissance.

4 *BM*, XIX, chapter VIII.

150

It is the offer of a series of experiences and values conveyed by the educators' testimonies and by the accompaniment of those who love and are loved. While Don Bosco was happy to use the term 'familiarity' to define how the relationship between educators and young people should be, he went further than that: "You cannot have love without this familiarity, and where this is not evident there can be no confidence."[5] Familiarity is not simply a methodological means or resource but is the result of a highly positive regard for the young person: kind parenting will then be the real and daily way of relating to one another; sincere mutual affection will create spontaneous and frank social environments; the person will be treated as an individual, on an equal footing, even if he or she is actively part of a network or a group.

The above considerations have a special application in a particular Salesian praxis: 'Salesian assistance',[6] considered as a method, but above all as an attitude. 'Salesian assistance' is an expression of friendship, discreet but incisive, effective and affective, of the educator with the young inside and outside the classroom, the workshop, the group and other regulated spaces. It is not intimidating or invasive surveillance. With Salesian assistance, the Preventive System entrusts educational effectiveness to the encouraging presence of the educator.

Don Bosco was a specialist in 'the first encounter' with the young; indeed, these moments are narrated by him, relived and proposed as an educational norm. Salesian education must therefore be understood not only in terms of provision, but also in terms of presence. In this regard, a few considerations should be made about this assistance:

• It is primarily a direct encounter, a physical presence among the young people[7] and therefore a contact with their lives and their interests;

5   *Letter from Rome.*
6   Cf. J. Rodríguez, *Sobre las huellas de Don Bosco. Algunas reflexiones sobre la asistencia salesiana,* (Bogotá: Giro, 1999). (new ed.).
7   "When we want to show someone Benedictine spirituality, we take them to the 'monastery'. If we want to directly experience the high point of Focolarine spirituality, we invite them to the 'Mariapolis'. To see Salesian spirituality up close, live and direct, you have to go to the playground and observe the Salesians among and with the young people" (J. E. Vecchi, *Rasgos de la espiritualidad salesiana,* (Madrid: CCS, 2000), 140).

it must not be forgotten that the educator loves what the learners love, sympathetically appreciates their world and is attentive to their real needs.

• Instead of a formal and distant approach, it is a friendly presence, where young people see interpersonal communication as a matter of course, because their educators are like parents, siblings and friends.

• It is an active presence with moral force and encourages differentiated initiatives, individual and environmental initiatives, aimed at awakening and fostering certain essential skills, such as emotional and creative skills.

• Finally, it is to bear witness with one's own life, because the values taught by the educator, if they are transmitted in their behaviour and in their open dialogue, cannot fail to attract the attention of young people and to raise questions in them.

4. But this pedagogy of winning hearts and making oneself loved also pays special attention to a demanding love that pushes one to embody values, translating them into a sense of duty and responsibility, positively reinforcing one's commitments on the path of growth and goodness. Don Bosco did not want the young people in the Salesian house to be treated with sentimentality, naive psychology or patronised: he corrects and warns, insists on commitment, on good moral conduct, taking care to form the heart, mind and habits. He speaks and writes to them in a concise way, advises them, invites them to make resolutions for a human and spiritual life. He follows the particularly significant wisdom of his mother, Mamma Margaret, his first teacher and mentor.

He also uses the mistakes, blunders, acts of misconduct or conflict as an educational tool. Disciplinary intervention does not have a punitive function, but is a moment of individual and group awareness, a re-establishment of a reasonable order with a view to peaceful coexistence; an active incentive for the assumption of active co-responsibility for the good of all. Everything has been thought of and considered as an educational 'family' and following a 'family spirit'.

5. An educational-pastoral community is something organic, it has to grow, which implies the necessity to invest time. For this reason, it seems evident that we need to accompany each of the members of the educational-pastoral community. We return once again to discuss the extraordinary educational adventure that we call 'accompaniment'.

From its origins, the educational-pastoral model has developed this accompaniment in various ways. perspectives and times, it seems to us that they can be grouped into three categories: accompaniment by means of the environment, by means of groups and personally. These different aspects are a formative mediation and coexist in each educational-pastoral community.

The objective of personal accompaniment (at an intensive or a normal pace) as an educational process is one-to-one. The Salesian educational-pastoral style is obliged to offer occasions and real possibilities for face-to-face dialogue, in which communication is neither impeded nor hurried. The life of the members of an educative-pastoral community is not exhausted by the environment or the group, even if the experiences are decisive.

In speaking specifically of accompanying young people, we are reaffirming the importance of illuminating the light of inner integrity in the person, helping to build one's own life project, which is indispensable for personal and Christian maturity. Accompanying must lead to the discovery of one's own needs and wounds, to an encounter and to reconciliation with oneself. It also awakens active collaboration on the path of one's own growth, stimulates the internalisation of everyday experiences, encourages discussion and a constructive critical attitude.

In this area, the practice of individual meetings and conversations is becoming more and more important. The times and rhythms are not the same for everyone, and the contents are not even the same. Respect for a person's rhythm, speed and pauses is fundamental: they are different in each person and demand patience, perseverance and belief in the possibility of change.

In every educational-pastoral Salesian presence or service there are multiple possibilities of individual communication, a varied repertoire of spontaneous and informal moments; but these more systematic ones are indispensable. Among them, spiritual accompaniment is a pedagogical-spiritual journey that refers to Jesus and his Good News as a way of seeing and interpreting reality. From this perspective, one is helped to discern one's personal life project in the Church and in the world, and to grow constantly in the spiritual life to the point of holiness.

Care for the personal dimension guarantees life-giving opportunities, i.e., it offers a space, affectively rich but respectful of freedom, which allows the person to "breathe", to question themselves, to exercise their own responsibility; an opportunity in which to find help to be able to be patiently in control of themselves. In fact, this is a demand that entails two conditions in every educational-pastoral community: on the one hand, to guarantee adequate space and time to carry out this service, understanding that this appeal to personal dialogue must be seen as an important resource and as an undoubtedly educational opportunity; on the other hand, there is an ever more urgent need for people who are ready to listen and to be attentive to the requirements of the people who are in need, to welcome confidences with respect and clarity, without ever invading the privacy of personal conscience. There is a need for accompaniers, guides, competent educational figures who have the gift of listening, who know how to be open to the truth of young people and who accept the educational responsibility of assisting young people and educators.

2.2. Parish that evangelises (religious experience and the evolving pedagogy)

We would now like to refer to the design of a series of proposals that are adapted and diversified to the lives of the recipients, which aim, in some cases, to teach them religious literacy; in others, to help them discover and achieve their Christian vocation.

1. As we saw earlier, every Salesian environment must develop and propose values that give substance to all the aspects of the Salesian model. Now, at this point, we give an account of the most relevant ideas and arguments concerning the cultivation of internalisation, as the first step towards knowing oneself, accepting oneself and meeting oneself, others and God. In this step, any proposal must be careful to ensure the gradual, continuous and sequential nature of the process.

For Don Bosco, in fact, the path to the summit of piety is directed by a practical education, a pedagogy of small goals that takes into account the psychological reality of the young people and begins with simple things. Short, positive steps in duty, in study, in work and in ordinary life have a great impact on the young person's personality in the medium and long term. The Salesian does not want the young person to set unattainable ideals or goals and, consequently, to make titanic efforts to achieve them. On many occasions, the young person's efforts could fall short and what they have objectively achieved is not valued as a success; in this case they are left with the unpleasant feeling of a new failure.

For this reason, times of spiritual 'recharging' are important to keep the enthusiasm alive, distributed in the daily, weekly, monthly and annual rhythms. This dynamic also marked the rhythms of the community of Valdocco, a climate of 'permanent formation' that generally culminated in a celebration.

We help young people to recognise attitudes typical of a religious experience: admiration, contemplation, the discovery of the greatness of simple things and a love of the nature that the Creator has placed in our path, openness to the world, a sense of gratitude and prayer. It is also important to make room for silence, which can mute so many distracting elements that do not help us to listen to the heart and to life. A silence that has to do with recovering intimacy and identity, with opening a door to spirituality and interior growth. Some have spoken of the 'pedagogy of awakening' to the most hidden realities, to recognise signs and messages, to be open to the sense of God present in these manifestations.

Today we need to promote the development of the religious dimension of the person, both of Christians and of those who belong to other religions, deepening it, purifying it and opening it to the desire for a further journey of faith. In the case of the Christian faith, to evangelise is to accompany the discovery of Jesus Christ in the small universe of each young person, in the garden of their daily life, of their being, knowing, appreciating, deciding and committing themselves. To make one see with one's own eyes that each one has been created big enough to contain God himself; to learn to say: "How beautiful it is to know that God the Father loves me and cares for me!"

In the same vein, let us remember that the Preventive System is also a 'narrated' spirituality, an experience that transcends daily witness and educational passion; this requires the establishment of communities of believers in which the experience of faith is visible and credible: communities that are affable, close, deep, tenaciously committed and open to all young people who are seeking their path in life; a solid home environment, an image of a Church that is fresh, attractive, active, capable of responding to the expectations of young people; therefore, it is necessary to look up and see an educational environment with people who live an authentic vocation.

In this regard, we borrow the eloquent words of George Steiner, an internationally renowned teacher, who asserts that in the school setting, "if a student perceives that you are in some way possessed by what you teach, that is a first step. He may not agree; ...but he will listen; it is the miraculous moment when dialogue with a passion begins to be established."[8]

2. In every educational-pastoral community, care is taken of the liturgical seasons and the Christian celebration of daily events. In the Salesian educational process, a specific, graded and singularised weight is attributed to the means of grace, especially the Blessed Sacrament, Reconciliation and the Eucharist, which in Don Bosco's mind were the pillars that should support the formative framework. Particular attention is given to initiation and conscious and active participation in the celebration and particularly to the role of faith in the community, which emanates from the memory and the presence of the Lord and is celebrated in the sacraments of Christian initiation.

In the celebration of these sacraments, preparation is fostered by a welcoming and friendly atmosphere that encourages openness of heart; care is taken with the language and the message so that it leads to a true personal relationship with Christ through the beauty and depth that it communicates; it promotes a personal commitment to live what has been celebrated in daily life.

3. Of extreme importance is the encounter and interaction with the Word of God. The biblical text comes through preaching and proclamation, through catechesis, through liturgical-sacramental celebration and through the artistic and cultural expression of the people. In the Salesian approach to living the faith, the Word of God is the content of faith; the festive celebration, the space of expression; prayer, the conducive atmosphere; communication and music its style.

The catechetical (content) and teaching (method) richness of the Word in youth celebrations are very important educationally, as are the formative

---

8   G. Steiner & C. Ladjali, *Elogio de la transmision*, [4th ed.], (Madrid: Siruela, 2016), 116.

efforts and the integration of the Word in all these elements. Young people are increasingly sensitive to the prayerful reading of the Word of God in the form of *lectio divina* when the biblical text is adapted in a language that is appropriate for them and connects with their life.

4. In general terms, with spiritual accompaniment, the careful practice of prayer and the pedagogy of the personal life project, discernment towards responsible choices gradually matures. In the same way, those experiences of education in the faith that help young people to service and apostolic commitment are part of the Salesian style. Don Bosco urged us not to neglect religious practices and helped us to live them in a more fraternal and supportive world, starting from the very nature of his Oratory. For this reason, it is necessary to offer young people experiences of service for the benefit of humanity that help them to personally integrate their faith with their lives, becoming, according to the possibilities of each one, witnesses and evangelisers. It is about a faith that stimulates and deepens the processes of humanisation and promotion of individuals and groups, according to the model of Jesus Christ.

It is necessary that young people feel concerned by the poor, assuming a critical analysis and affective and effective implications both on a personal and group level. It is necessary that every commitment be full of real people and urgent commitments in the face of emerging social situations. Giving life, motivating hope to this world of ours where death—both human and environmental—leaves many traces of pain and suffering.

We can also say that openness to the missionary vocation and the social commitment of charity in the voluntary sector are mature expressions of education to the faith. At the present time, this Salesian voluntary service includes substantially large areas of intervention: culture, social assistance, recreation, cooperative development, group animation, training of catechists and pastoral workers. In its various forms, the volunteer assumes a mentality and a testimony of the highest moral and social value.

This apostolic dynamism is not born as an isolated event: it is the extension of the identity of every Christian, it is its natural 'blossoming'. The social dimension of charity belongs to the education of a person who is socially and politically committed to justice, to the building of a more just and humane society, discovering in it a fully evangelical inspiration. The proposal and witness of social awareness through projects and campaigns of solidarity give credibility to the Gospel proclamation, thus expressing its capacity to humanise.

2.3. School that prepares for life (holistic growth through education)

The considerations of this third point are manifold. In the first place, the image of 'school' speaks of those resources necessary for each young person to grow in a harmonious, creative and original way to realise their potential, i.e., optimum development of all areas of their personality.

1. A good structure of values is the backbone of any educational approach, understood as ideal models of personal fulfilment. Value is that which makes something worthy of being appreciated, wanted and sought after in order to reach the ideal model of behaviour and life. Values play the role of guiding and directing human conduct; attitudes, on the other hand, are their crystallisation.

Values education is not 'teaching' values; it is above all cultivating everything that makes it possible for young people to grasp, appreciate and assimilate the values present in the analysed and substantiated facts. This set of values acts as a compass for decisions, since they are the usual reference point to consider options, especially in moments of doubt, conflict or choice. Given the importance and relevance of values, the experience of these values is more than a simple notional knowledge; they must be integrated on an affective level, tested in some way, recognised existentially. The intellectual path alone is insufficient to assure that one possesses one or other value.

If values become regulators of individual behaviour, if they are a motive for action, a young person is cooperative not because they know the importance of the value of cooperation or because circumstances force them to collaborate with others, but because they feel the need to help and serve others in a selfless way. Collaboration, in this case, becomes a motive for action. It is necessary to restructure and modify one's own attitudes, and this, logically, requires time and practise.

2. Secondly, this symbol of the 'school' obliges us to teach, accompany and facilitate meaningful experiences, combining those that we can describe as particularly intense with more everyday ones. This involves making sense of what happens every day, their ordinary and natural concerns (for their studies or work and for their family), obligations (school, family and work burdens or responsibilities), anxieties (nervousness, complexes, insecurities, resistances) or relationships (attachments and detachments, affection and disaffection, fears and distrust).

To be more precise, we will refer to a daily practice introduced by Don Bosco in the Oratory, the 'good night'. This custom has been extended in Salesian environments through the 'good morning' or 'good evening',[9] an expression of a warm daily welcome or farewell to the young people. This moment, designed educationally by Don Bosco, consisted in taking a fact or an event that helped the pupils to think about the topic, reflect on consequences, draw conclusions and recommend ways of approaching it. It was a personalised practice expressed in a lifelong lesson; its purpose was, and still is, to give meaning to daily events, daily activities and relationships, instructing how to live a wise and virtuous life.

It can be said that one of the things that ensured the smooth running of the Oratory was this little word every night. We can say that the Salesian model adopted the ministry of the 'word', the main communicative tool for speaking to the heart in an understandable and thought-provoking language.

3. The map of these interventions is completed by the coming together of all educational interventions for the formation of strong identities, of unified personalities: an operative option in which all contributions, well prioritised, are integrated and mutually reinforced. The Salesians believe that the educational-pastoral model can help to form young people with sufficiently strong and coherent personalities; they are pressed by the urgency of reconciling and structuring those fragmented aspects of the young person's life, a consequence of the wounds in their personal story.

In this sense, it is necessary to form stable attitudes and structures in the personality of young people, such as the concepts of self-esteem, self-

---

9   Cf. F. Acosta, 'Las buenas noches en el marco del Proyecto Educativo Pastoral Salesiano', in *Misión Joven* 78–79 (1983), 21–34.

confidence, socialisation, participation, autonomy, the acquisition of values and responsibility. All these elements, and others that we could add, have the ability to influence personality, they are absolutely necessary for a positive and healthy development that allows individuals to act as free and discerning people. Here, we would also highlight the impact of life skills, i.e., the use of appropriate higher-order competencies for problem solving in personal, family, group or work-related issues.

4. We do not want to move on without referring, by way of example, to the importance in the Salesian model of physical activity and sport in education as a formula for play and healthy group entertainment. It is also worth recalling the ample space and dignity given by the Salesian tradition to these moments: not only does it reinforce the personal relationship, as an authentic school of physical health and mental wellbeing; it is also an excellent ground for the promotion and development of self-control, sociability, discipline, creativity and assimilation. The same can be said of play in general: it educates free association, imagination, role-playing and the absorbing of norms of coexistence. In both cases, from the Salesian educational point of view, the emphasis is on the socialisation of the person and not only on the competitive component.

5. An essential element to emphasise is to accompany young people in the development and maturing of their emotional and sexual world. It is imperative to consider the educational approach to this area, to deal with it without piecemeal strategies. In practice, an arbitrary approach leads to ambivalence, and thus to distortions, to inadequate and often disturbing perceptions of the personality and the loving bond between people.

There is no doubt that an adequate understanding of affective-sexuality and love is necessary in the holistic development of children and young people. Indeed, the emotional experience colours the subjective perception of reality, it is the guiding criterion of the relational path and of ethical evaluation, although it often runs parallel to rationality. Affection and sexuality tend to evoke each other on many occasions. In whatever way sexuality and affection come to meet, both influence and condition each other.

The affective and sexual domain encompasses biological as well as moral and spiritual aspects of the personality. Too many places contribute to the discrediting of this area and its frivolous use. The degradation and impoverishment of some sex education programmes has led to the subject being placed outside the emotional development of the person and, therefore, disconnected from the capacity to love and to ethically value actions.

A convergent educational effort is needed—multi and interdisciplinary— that helps, through specific programmes, to verbalise the interior world, to constructively manage emotions, feelings, sexual drives, and to live love as an experience of growth that promotes and stimulates the passage from a self-centred, infantile or possessive love to an interpersonal, supportive love. The holistic education of the person will lead young people to appreciate the authentic values of affectivity (respect for oneself and for others, the dignity of the person, transparency in relationships, fidelity) and human sexuality as a determining value in the path of maturity.

In accordance with what has been said above, it is necessary to accept a comprehensive and positive conception of sexuality and affectivity in the re-dimensioning of personal love and self-giving, with a calm acceptance of limits, with the acquisition of motives and criteria for self-regulation.

Generally speaking, educators and those who have experience in the formation of pre-adolescents and young people know how much inner strength they have and how much sincere enthusiasm they are capable of. They seek, among other things, transparent relationships in the family, with educators, with friends, with colleagues, in the work environment; relationships that help them to feel good and to calmly proceed in the realisation of their own personal journey. We take care, therefore, of environments rich in communicative and affective exchanges. On the other hand, accompanying families is an educational challenge that we must face, contributing the characteristics proper to the Salesian charism: familiarity, constant availability for dialogue and closeness.

6. The next point to be dealt with, and which is crucial in the ordinary life of educational institutions, is discipline. Every formator has to be qualified in relational skills and, at the same time, know how to exist in spaces of uncertainty with continuous surprises, able to face with serenity the conflicts that all growth entails. The balance between kindness and constraint, between consideration for the person and appropriate order, between familiarity and authority, make discipline a sign of the competence of a team of educators.

It is a matter of educating not with repression and punishment, but with respect for the personality, the will and the freedom of the learner.

In this chapter of discipline and maintaining good order, the Salesian educational style has always had pedagogical criteria at its core. In fact, the Salesian educational-pastoral model developed some particular criteria for correction to be educational:

• First of all, to use all means before punishing, not to go immediately to what seems most obvious, to what solves the problem of order, to what is convenient and quick (discipline is necessary, but its purpose is the good of the young person).

• Secondly, the punishment that truly educates is the one that helps to change behaviour in a positive sense, awakening the inner resources of reason and affection; well-administered punishment makes the response more conscious and freer; that is why only temporary and moral sanctions are educational; never physical ones.

• Thirdly, one must know how to choose the right moment for the young person and for the educator; it is counter-educational if the punishment expresses revenge or violence on the part of the educator, since in both cases it humiliates and offends the learner.

• A fourth criterion, to act taking into account the situation of the person rather than the fault, helping them to overcome their difficulties, avoiding further damage, preventing the harm from undermining the educational environment.

• Finally, that the young person knows what will be reasonably demanded of him or her and that educators are united in their criteria and actions.

7. Another point to emphasise is to work simultaneously on humanistic and professional competence, so that young people can enter the world of work as highly qualified citizens. To equip young people intellectually is to give them 'content', to free them from ignorance, to give them the tools to carry out a decent job and to train them in all the essential elements for the development of the "good Christian and honest citizen" of Don Bosco.

This phrase expresses three complementary objectives. On the one hand, professionalism should lead to work being carried out with a sense of duty, competence and real satisfaction, aware of the limits of the world of work, conscious of one's own contribution to social growth. It thus responds to a deep concern for the dignity of work and diligence in the fulfilment of duty. Work is not simply a mere commercial matter where the result of what is generated produces a certain profitability. It is about training the mind with the acquisition of operational skills for a profession, the training of a sense of initiative and entrepreneurial talent, the serious undertaking of commitments and the responsibility of doing a job well in the realm of daily work.

For Don Bosco, work is not understood only as a task to be carried out as an aspect of social organisation: it is preparing for life, being able to earn one's living honestly.

Secondly, we cannot fail to mention that work is an indicator of integral growth: the duties of daily life and daily work humanise the person and make him or her a sharer in God's creative work, develop his or her abilities and talents, discarding frivolity and contributing to the transformation of future societies. Through work, young people give expression to their dreams, identify their hopes, accept their achievements as their own and face challenges with courage.

As far as Don Bosco was concerned, work is the key to the formation of professional habits, of personal effort and responsibility for any educational plan (through the routines and work schedule). The aim is to articulate the meaning of integration into the labour market along three lines: religious-moral orientation, intellectual orientation and professional orientation. Vocational training is tailored towards the acquisition of specific skills inherent to the profession, focused on professional versatility. But it also emphasises the acquisition of personal competencies or, in other words, attention to the person and his or her way of life. It is a matter of combining 'horizonal' skills, specific to the professional sector, with skills that we could call 'vertical', such as self-expression, self-realisation of interpersonal and social relationships.

Thirdly, the concept of professional life in a Salesian centre is directed towards ethical awareness and responsibility in the service of society. The Salesian model for the world of vocational training prepares for the future by connecting both aspects: the personal and the communal aspects. This confidence in the educational efficacy of work—individually and socially—inspired the work of Don Bosco from the very beginning of the Oratory.

8. All forms and expressions of artistic communication such as theatre,[10] music, film, photography, literature, dance and urban art are also educational tools. Not only do they enrich and express an artistic repertoire, but they also have a higher educational potential. Salesian pedagogy is always attentive to these initiatives, aware that in many environments young people are best reached through non-formal activities. The Salesian model thus promotes the ability to relate and integrate new and innovative responses.

Recognising their strong social and educational value, this type of expression provides some very significant aptitudes:

• They present their own unique possibility of approaching reality and interpreting it, using aesthetic language and symbols; they are an altruistic way of generating ideas and feelings, they encourage free expression and reveal fundamental aspects of human experience that would be difficult to express in other ways.

• They are a unique contribution to the development of intellectual, creative and expressive skills, training young people in concentration, curiosity, discipline and perseverance.

• They offer a space for personal relationships: through their various manifestations, they create spaces for socialising, collaboration and fun.

• They are a unique means for evangelisation, proclamation and expression of the Good News; music and art encourage the preservation of the celebratory space and its festive character.

The use of these different aesthetic languages—rhythmic, musical and poetic—stimulates the appreciation of beauty and activates a progressive enrichment of one's own expressive heritage and the capacity to love what is beautiful. It leads the young person to contemplation, admiration, critical ability and flexibility of judgement. Listening becomes more than an auditory perception, it becomes a language of imagery: educating for beauty means

10   Cf. T. Lewicki, 'Educazione estetica. I recenti sviluppi a confronto con la tradizione educativa salesiana e la prassi contemporanea', in Orlando (ed.), *Con Don Bosco, educatori dei giovani del nostro tempo*, 412–430. The author highlights, as an example, how well known and studied is Don Bosco's intuition and teaching on the educational value of the theatre and how he introduced it in the daily life of his educational institutions. He himself is an adaptor-writer of plays, providing an excellent example for Salesian educators.

involving the whole range of sensitivity and emotions, imagination and creativity, the ability to express 'beautifully' one's own sensations and feelings and to understand the expression of others. For this reason, music and singing were two original ways of recreating the oratorian atmosphere created by Don Bosco in Valdocco. This artistic experience evokes the grace and the depth of all human beings, which allows openness to transcendence.

9. The final element in this framework is the educational interest in the new information and communication technologies.[11] To the classical educational environments we must now add the environment of technological media. In recent years, virtual spaces such as social networks, video games and chat rooms have inevitably replaced traditional functions of public engagement, helping to create a common perspective and a new structuring of interpersonal relations and communication; they have created a space for instantaneous and universal communication.

The upsurge of these realities is like a wave that is sweeping practically everyone and everything along; it is bringing about a revolution in a multitude of social and personal contexts, becoming defining features of our most advanced societies. If technology is involved in the major issues of our time, education cannot be detached from this new reality. Everything is happening online, and the young generations—the 'digital natives', cyberkids, click generation— have acquired a high capacity for immediate access to it and have developed the skills to use it. It is, however, a new educational challenge for the Salesian approach, marked by an unstoppable advance and innovation that is surprising for its rapid growth and its unlimited educational possibilities.[12]

---

11   Cf. Ch. Giaccardi, 'Giovani, media digitali e sfide educative', in Orlando (ed.), *Con Don Bosco, educatori dei giovani del nostro tempo*, 70–76. The contribution of this sociologist, a lecturer at the Catholic University of Sacro Cuore (Milan), is very interesting, as she insists that the digital environment is not opposed to the real one, but rather an extension of it. Digital relationships are no less authentic than real ones but offer us new possibilities of protagonism and witness. For educators, the digital environment is a risk, but also an opportunity to be seized. She insists that we must overcome the prejudices of technological determinism, digital dualism and the generation gap.

12   The social psychologist Dolors Reig refers to the expression "augmented society", see D. Reig, *Socionomía: ¿vas a perderte la revolución social?* (Barcelona: Deusto, 2012). To define it, she sets out three aspects of the use of technology, namely: technologies for information and communication (ICT), technologies for ▷

The speed of information and the possibility of finding profiles with whom to share interests are just some of the positive aspects of social networks. Another benefit is the easy access to all kinds of tips, resources, guides, tutorials and manuals. Since the Internet entered our daily lives, distances, time and costs have been reduced. It opens up a wide field of initiatives for didactic, educational and cultural activities, for the Christian animation of youth groups, for catechesis and for prayer.

Consequently, the emergence of this technological universe creates culture and shapes mentalities in the interactive generation of young people. Such a culture brings with it new knowledge, new ways of accessing culture and new languages. We are going through a period of profound technological revolution in which not only a new vision of socio-cultural reality is being born, but also a vision that is shaping in the minds of individuals new forms of socialisation, relationship, exchange, conceptualisation and collective identification. We live with a generation of young people who have adopted technology as another part of their lives on which to build their identity and their way of being in the world.

Professors Howard Gardner and Katie Davis address the three crucial areas of young people's lives affected by the networked world: identity, intimacy and imagination.[13]

In short, the approach to technology is an important step not only because of new communication, social and recreational possibilities, but also in the journey of growth and affirmation of one's own identity. This information ecosystem and its effects influence the development of young people's personalities, their choice of basic values and their position before God and

---

learning and knowledge (TAC) and technologies for empowerment and participation (TEP). These three functionalities make the use of technology possible and ultimately dependent on the attitude that we as individuals adopt.

13   Cf. H. Gardner & K. Davis, *The App Generation. How Today's Youth Navigate Identity, Intimacy, and Imagination in a Digital World*, (London: Yale University Press, 2014). The authors reveal the benefits and drawbacks of apps: on the one hand, they foster a sense of identity, on the other, they blur it; they foster deep relationships and, at the same time, weaken them; finally, they stimulate creativity and, at other times, hinder creative imagination.

humankind. Often, these media assume the role of the 'hidden educator'[14] in the formation of young people, proposing what is excellent, both aesthetically and morally. The technology user simultaneously assumes the roles of consumer and producer of content. Their incisive effectiveness and their increasingly widespread presence make these media a true and authentic alternative school for broad sectors of the world's population, especially for young people and the general public.

However, the other side of the coin of this era of online[15] connectivity and reality, is the lack of privacy, the defencelessness of minors and the constant exposure of personal lives to third parties; the speed with which pseudo-information spreads (false myths, unverified opinions, fabricated stories or fake news) and the 'FOMO' phenomenon (the 'fear of missing out' on something).

The challenge for the future is the creation of new training pathways appropriate to the current situation in order to be able to manage the high rate of innovation that ICT presents today. Education must provide the means, environments and processes to develop not only digital skills: it must raise awareness of the possible consequences of one's actions for oneself and for others. Hence the interest at this point in promoting an education focused not only on the beneficial use of the Internet, but also on the user's commitment to his or her own ethical conscience.

2.4. Playground to meet friends and live cheerfully (the pedagogy of joy and celebration)

One of the key factors of pedagogical success is the experience of the 'playground', a broad concept linked to the theme of 'family life'. It refers

---

14   P. Bignardi, 'Cambiamenti social enti e sfide educative, in Orlando (ed.), *Con Don Bosco, educatori dei giovani del nostro tempo*, 54. Prof. Bignardi, professor at the Pontifical Salesian University, also adds two elements that challenge educational processes: the crisis of the adult generation and the weakness of the places where young people come together.

15   In our case, **online** reputation is the image of young people on the Internet. Beyond the image projected by the individual, online reputation is also composed of the news, comments and opinions expressed by third parties in social networks, forums, blogs and online media.

to an environment in which many free spaces for living together, relaxing, recharging and celebrating are valued.

The experience of the 'playground' is a call to leave formal structures, the limits of traditional spaces, to make recreation, play sport, engage in healthy competition or excursions, a place rich in fun educational opportunities.

1. In all of these places there is a balance between what is planned and what is spontaneous; they have a strong capacity for influence, they create positive relationships and informal positive environments. They all include aesthetic and symbolic elements, languages and youth resources through which educational accomplishments and the value of individuals are visualised. They also facilitate and give a homely tone and feel of family life, providing essential and beneficial opportunities for interaction. They are not educational embellishments that are ultimately dispensable. They are places of spontaneity and relationships: as simple in expression as they are effective in results.

For these reasons, it is necessary to focus on those times and spaces where the educator-youth relationship goes beyond the formality of other structures, environments and stereotypical roles. In the words of Don Bosco: "The teacher who is seen only in the classroom is a teacher and nothing more, but if he participates in the recreation of the children, he also becomes a brother."

The 'playground' is all those spaces and times in where the attentive and genuine Salesian gaze towards young people dwells, without being stigmatising, without being overwhelming, capable of approaching their daily contexts and understanding their situation as a first step towards any intervention. The playground is an open book: it is an excellent means—if not the best means— to diagnose the essential Salesian educational perceptions, to listen to what is going on, to decipher the problems and interests, to explain the "whys and wherefores" of what is happening. It is there that we get to know the young person in his or her peer group and discover all his or her natural qualities.

The holiday season, and especially the autumn walks, offered Don Bosco this precious opportunity. It was a strategy with a real educational intention that broke the usual routine of the day and put the young students in direct contact with life, the richness of traditions, cultural, religious and moral values, the people of the countryside, the beauty of the agricultural landscapes, the art and iconography of the churches and monuments. In the course of the walk, they took the opportunity to enjoy some local festivals and liturgical celebrations, accompanying the procession with the education of theatre, music and song. But the walks were essentially Don Bosco himself, his paternal affection; with the young people, he travelled along roads, through villages and rural areas.

2. Another of the most effective educational devices is the collaborative group. Through it, young people are accompanied by reconciling their various concerns, giving them the opportunity to experiment, to be involved, to invent and to re-express initiatives. Groups and associations of various kinds are therefore 'the work of the young'. Although they are driven by educators, who stimulate them through their action, the real empowerment comes from the young people who participate in these groups and who take responsibility for their management in their own way.

For young people, educational associations can be the place where their hopes come into contact with values and, because they are involved in discovering them, they assimilate them in their lives. They thus allow young people to shape values with the corresponding cultural concepts to which they are most sensitive. Don Bosco himself, guided by his intuition of the soul of the young, discovered in practice the great opportunity offered by groups and associations. Adapting to the diverse and multiple needs of his boys, he created various forms of association for them, such as the 'societies'.[16]

The groups constitute a mediation in the midst of the masses, where there is a danger of anonymity and loneliness. The creation of these group environments allows young people to meet comfortably, with the confidence to express their opinions. The group is a network of meaningful encounters, of identified stories, of quality human relationships that are neither just practical

---

16   Before Bishop Fransoni (1852) appointed Don Bosco spiritual director in charge of the three Oratories in Turin and thus opened a new chapter in the history of the Oratory, an important event took place: the creation of the first youth societies, in response to the needs expressed by the young people themselves. The first youth organisation he conceived was the 'Company of St Louis', founded in 1847, whose purpose was to promote the religious practices and Christian service of its members among the boys of the Oratory. Then, in 1849, Don Bosco founded the 'Society of Mutual Help', an association of young apprentices established within the Society of St Louis as an insurance against temporary unemployment or illness.

nor standardised. The community and what is communal can only become a reference if they represent a meaningful and friendly space, a living and affective group that is not simply functional.

What is significant in this associative group profile is the recognition and acceptance of the diversity of others, a sign of companionship. This dynamic is an almost obligatory step towards developing an experience of community. Through a variety of youth groups and associations, we can encourage young people to a meaningful experience of ecclesial life.

3. We have spoken in other sections about joy, the 'first commandment' for Don Bosco. Let us recall the metaphor for this joy is the feast day, celebrated at various times, carefully distributed throughout the Oratory year as stages of a formative journey. Typical of the Salesian atmosphere is the excitement of celebrations prepared and celebrated with all the necessary energy and personal and community commitment, accompanied by music, outdoor settings and ceremonies. The Salesian educational-pastoral model has complete confidence in this educational resource.

In short, the playground is the main stage for joy and freedom; they are twin sisters who are born and work together, and whose intervention makes it possible to express what words cannot express; they become the oxygen of the relationships that are embodied in Valdocco. Don Bosco believed in a climate of freedom, that the children should run, jump, shout and play. It was never understood as absolute spontaneity, but as freedom incarnated in an educational environment. In fact, among the seven guidelines that explain the success of the Oratory, and which Don Bosco enumerated in 1875, one is precisely this: "Joy, singing, music and great freedom in games."

For this reason, at the Don Bosco Oratory, we sing and learn music; we teach catechism and live the practices of piety; we hold classes, set up workshops, look for work for apprentices; we organise excursions and theatre performances. It is a world tailored to the needs of the young people, where they can find free and appropriate answers to their needs and desires.

Chapter Seven

Scenarios of the Salesian Educational-Pastoral Model

1. A Multitude of Possibilities for an Educational Dream

The mosaic of Salesian environments and services for young people shows that the educational-pastoral model is continually being updated. It responds to new needs through a variety of works and projects, from the university level to community and technical education, formal and non-formal education.

When St John Bosco was nine years old, he had a dream that left its mark on him for the rest of his life. According to various specialists in his 'Biographical Memoirs', where more than 150 dreams of Don Bosco are narrated, this would be the first dream-revelation that would mark the beginning of what is today the Salesian work. Through his dreams he told the young people of the Oratory and his first Salesians appealing stories full of images and with strong educational and spiritual applications. When he tried to fall asleep, his mind would think of children, dream of projects and give shape to his vocation and his mission towards the poorest young people.

Being aware of the many needs of the world, the Salesians, over the years, have focused their efforts to make these dreams come true. Today, the Salesian educational-pastoral model is drawn in the image of those ideals and projects.

Although not exhaustive, the following are some reflections on the most important characteristics of the works and services developing the model today. They are made up of the places, projects, people and procedures managed according to the Salesian educational-pastoral model. The oratory-youth centre, the school and vocational training centre, the Salesian presence in higher education, the parish and church entrusted to the Salesians and the social works and services for young people at risk are briefly outlined.

We will describe the other works and services with which we try to reach out to young people and respond to the new challenges they present to us. Many of these new educational and pastoral situations are also present in the traditional works and are a sign of renewal and pastoral development.

> We carry out our mission mainly through activities and works where we are able to promote the Christian and social education of young people: such as the oratory and the youth centre, the school and the vocational centres, the residential homes and the houses for young people in difficulty. In parishes and missionary residences, we contribute to the spread of the Gospel and the welfare of the people, collaborating in the pastoral care of the local church with the riches of a specific vocation. Through specialised centres we offer our pedagogical and catechetical service in the youth sector. In the retreat houses we provide for the Christian formation of groups, especially of young people. We also dedicate ourselves to any other work whose purpose is the salvation of young people.[1]

---

1   Cf. C, art. 42.

Let us now look at these different educational environments or structures in which the essential components of the Salesian proposal are embodied.[2]

2. The Salesian Oratory, Prototype of Salesian Work

The Oratory of St Francis de Sales in Valdocco was the first established work of Don Bosco. It is there, even today, that his personal imprint is found: his ideology became the educational criterion applied over the years; for this reason, it constitutes the matrix of Salesian pedagogy, the germinal element of the whole work, the educational-pastoral plan that gave rise to all the others.

The Salesian oratory-youth centre is a house open to adolescents and young people from the surrounding area: a physical place of reference. It aims to be a presence in the lives of young people, with attention to their needs and opportunities; a 'fulltime' house that extends throughout the week with personal interactions and complementary activities; a comprehensive educational-pastoral programme enriched by the family presence of the educators among the young people, in recreational and religious activities.

The oratory should fill the empty times of work and occupation in the life of a young person and saturate it with possibilities, joy, human and supernatural values, education and entertainment, instruction and edification.[3]

1. The oratory-youth centre is organised as an educational-pastoral community made up of young people, animators, families, collaborators and the religious community. All feel called to an active and responsible participation, according to each one's own role. Each oratory-youth centre is a real house with concrete and well-defined spaces in a family atmosphere, with a shared educational-pastoral approach and an adequate accompaniment of groups and individuals.

The oratory-youth centre is a welcoming environment, open to a wide variety of children and young people, especially those most in need, and with

---

2   We will follow the text from the *Salesian Youth Ministry. Frame of Reference*, Chapter VII.

3   Braido, *Preventing, not repressing: the educational system of Don Bosco*, 393.

influence on a broad social area. At the same time, it is a space especially suited for personal interaction, where the Salesian assistance of the educators to the young people, even outside the physical environment of the oratory-youth centre, in their living spaces is of paramount importance. As we have seen, this is the Salesian style of encouragement and educational intervention.

Right from the first meetings, the Salesian animator knows how to establish a dialogue with the young people in order to motivate them and involve them more and more, gradually making them co-responsible in the activities and in the group processes in which they participate. Since the time of Don Bosco, youth involvement has been a characteristic feature of the educational-pastoral community of the Salesian oratory-youth centre. The epicentre of the educational task is the young person, and around them a variety of activities and experiences; a coordinated and interconnected animation aimed at the participation of young people in the planning, implementation and review of activities.

The involvement of young people in these processes helps to overcome passive conformity and ignorance in social reality. Specifically, the neighbourhood and the city are an educational space, and therefore initiatives are put into place that help to understand the environments of child and youth exclusion in the area, to participate actively—and critically—in the social situations in which they live, and to open up opportunities to become involved in their world. In its relationship with the neighbourhood, the Oratorian community also knows how to engage in dialogue with the institutions in order to work in a network.

2. The educational-pastoral community in the oratories/youth centres shares the reality of the young people, makes their concerns, problems and expectations its own. With a flexible and creative management, it is able to adapt to the diversity and spontaneity typical of an oratorian education. It is certainly an educational and pastoral presence of significant reference in the world of young people, some of whom do not always succeed in integrating into other structures and other educational settings.

Although the historical development and the extension of Don Bosco's work have not altered the inspiring principles and characteristics of the Salesian oratory, the new socio-educational situations are a call for its modernisation. Salesian creativity and innovative spirit have always been an antidote to routine, immobility and conformity, responding to the new concepts of educational free time, a reality that is increasingly valued in our society as a space open to all kinds of social, cultural and sporting experiences; an area in which to develop social relations and personal skills.

In a situation where young people's free time is saturated by so many initiatives, the oratory has to pay attention to the style of relationships that last over time, to the quality of the approach, to the collaboration with the families. At the same time, we must pay attention to the ever-present risk of reducing the dynamics of the oratory-youth centre exclusively to leisure and recreational activities, allowing the disappearance of those initiatives of greater commitment and demand for young people available for a deeper formative path; that is, those that are in tune with the Christian educational approach that is Salesian youth spirituality.

With regards to associations and societies, a wide and articulated range of initiatives and groups have been established according to the interests of young people: spontaneous groups in which natural leaders and immediate interests prevail; defined groups, with specific formative itineraries according to the various sporting, cultural, socio-political, ecological, social communication, religious deepening, missionary awareness, internal animation and voluntary work environments.

3. Salesian oratories have been able to adapt to new situations in different ways, even taking on different names. In some contexts, 'oratory' is understood as a programme, whether festive or daily, intended especially for younger people and open to a broad group, with methodological approaches that encourage a variety of forms of free time and religious encounters in their environment. By 'youth centre' we mean a structure, intended above all for young people, open to all, with diversified initiatives for holistic growth, where the group methodology prevails, geared towards a Christian and social commitment. 'Oratory-youth centre' refers to an environment that includes both the open oratorian context and the commitment to more mature young people.

Many Salesian works are now oratory-youth centres that carry out various educational projects suitable for attracting and involving a wide range of people. These environments take on many forms and characteristics, depending on the different geographical, religious and cultural areas. There are, for example, night oratories, mobile presences for young people at risk, local or district oratories networked together, oratories that offer young people who are unemployed and outside the school system the possibility of acquiring basic training or preparing for the world of work; some also try to rehabilitate young people who are in a situation of serious social risk.

3. The School and the Vocational Training Centre: Specific Cultural Intervention for Education and Work Experience

Salesian schools and Salesian vocational training centres are two structures of formal training with their own related characteristics. There is no true Salesian school that does not prepare for work, nor is there a true Salesian technical centre that does not take into account the systematic development of culture.

Both entities are a vital means of formation, a valid element of grassroots outreach and a particularly effective means of evangelisation. They guide the cultural contents and the educational methodology according to a vision of humanity, of the world and of history inspired by the Gospel.

1. We recognise the fundamental value of vocational training and the school as places where culture is both assimilated and critically analysed, but also where the Gospel illuminates and questions it; this integration constitutes an important educational alternative in the current cultural, ethical and religious diversity of society. The socio-political and cultural reality, the new directions of school renewal in various countries and the intrinsic life of schools present new challenges and complex difficulties. It is necessary to specify criteria and strategies that, in the face of this complexity, guide the implementation of the Salesian educative and pastoral community.

In the same way as other areas, formal educational institutions are born from the Salesian educational-pastoral model to respond to the specific needs of young people and are part of a global project of education and evangelisation of young people. They also aim to contribute to the construction of a more just and dignified society for humankind.

For this reason, they have a number of specific characteristics: they try to be located in the most disadvantaged areas and give precedence to young people most in need; they denounce any discriminatory or exclusionary situations; they give priority to the development of all rather than the selection of the best; they promote a systematic civic and political training of their members; they become centres of animation and cultural and educational services for the improvement of the environment, preferably opting for curricula, specialisations and programmes that respond to the needs of the young people of the area; they practise closeness and solidarity through the availability of people and facilities, the offer of development services open to all, collaboration with other educational and social institutions; they promote a significant presence in the world of former students, so that they can be integrated in an active and proactive way in the cultural, educational and professional dialogue.

2. As we have already noted in Chapter Two, driven by the desire to guarantee the dignity and future of his young people, Don Bosco first of all established professional workshops, helping young people to find work and providing them with employment contracts to prevent them from being exploited. This is the matrix of today's vocational training centres, which are concerned with promoting the social, Christian and professional formation of young people. This scheme responds to the predispositions, abilities and perspectives of many of them whom, upon completion of basic training, aspire to enter the world of work. Vocational training is an effective instrument for holistic human development and the prevention of situations of risk for young people, as well as for Christian witness in social realities and in the development of the business world.

The organisation of these centres is fundamentally interdisciplinary and cross-cultural, which is necessary for the acquisition of the skills required in the world of work. Vocational training implies an education that is not a narrow profile, merely adjusted to the immediate needs of companies. On the contrary, the aim is to provide a broad education that combines specialisation with a solid personal, social and, where appropriate, transcendent education that enables students to be enterprising and to continue to develop in a comprehensive way throughout their lives.

In fact, the Salesians not only educate in the values inherent to work and scientific and technical fields, but also take care of the ethical and humanistic approach of each profession from the practical and day-to-day reality.

In this regard, it is vital to ensure training for employability, where young people are involved in a complex educational process in which, in addition to work-related skills, they learn the rights and duties of active citizenship; they experience social behaviour modelled on collaboration, individual responsibility and solidarity, and they structure their own identity in a way that is suitable for integration into the social and civil fabric.

Educators have an essential role to play in stimulating an entrepreneurial culture in young people, which is intimately linked to innovation, job creation, a positive response to challenges and even personal success.

3. Always attentive to the needs of young people, the Salesians broaden their commitment by promoting the school as a cultural interface for education, through which they can systematically respond to the needs of the developing age, the world, of people and of history.

From the point of view of schools, the growing trend towards specialisation of teachers and curricula, as well as the emphasis that education systems place on knowledge, often marginalises aspects related to the development of emotional, ethical and spiritual capacities in young people. The challenge for schools is to overcome the dissociation between the academic world and aspects of personal development, which, although included in the idea of a comprehensive education, can leave much to be desired in its realisation. Weaving the cognitive, affective and spiritual dimensions into the curriculum and into teaching practice requires time and pastoral intentionality.

It is necessary to understand that the main purpose of the school is to match teaching with life, to people's natural and social environment, and do so through a series of teaching approaches (conceptual, procedural and attitudinal) with which pupils can deal with and resolve everyday and familiar, changing and complex situations, in an ethical way.

The school, as a system, cannot become a mere cognitive learning tool that forgets about the real-life aspects of individuals. The meaning of 'educate' refers to that interaction between each young person and his or her context with the aim of exercising their personal and social potential to the full. In the words of Don Bosco: "Enlightening the mind to make the heart good."[4]

4. The educational-pastoral model is aimed at forming at the same time "honest citizens" and "good Christians", an identity card for those who recognise Don Bosco as an inspiring master of education. In fact, we cannot understand Salesian educational institutions without a clear commitment to evangelising education and to quality pastoral ministry. To this end, it is crucial that pastoral ministry become more and more integrated and widespread in the organisational culture of the educational centres, and that it be consciously and consistency present in the objectives of strategic and operative planning.

Therefore, in addition to offering explicit evangelising interventions, it is necessary that the whole architecture of the school prepares the personal, environmental and organisational conditions for this purpose. Pastoral ministry is a central option, embedded in the very heart of the teaching and non-teaching formative work. While it is necessary, it is not enough to draw up a framework or pastoral programme with structured initiatives: one key aspect, among others, is to ensure the identity of the teaching staff. In this sense, teachers and other educators closely involved in the school must be selected, integrated, trained and monitored with careful attention so that they can collaborate with creative loyalty in the educational-pastoral processes proper to a Salesian school.

The attitude of shared religious mission in the school is what makes it possible for every educational professional to be a witness of the Christian humanism that a Salesian school transmits. Today, more than ever, we need educational teams that are cohesive, identified, committed and congruent with the pedagogical style of the Salesian charism. Without a corporate identity, there is no shared mission.

---

4   G. Bosco, *Storia sacra per uso delle scuole utile ad ogni stato di persone*, (Turín: Speirani e Ferrero, 1847), 7.

5. There are also vocational training centres, also known as training centres for the world of work, with a particular formulation and implementation of a variety of options: guidance, teaching and training pathways, refresher courses, retraining, socio-occupational inclusion or reintegration, promotion of the social entrepreneurial fabric. They contribute to the personal progress of each individual and are aimed at a wide range of target groups: young people of compulsory school age; young people and adults looking for work; young people at risk or dropping out of school; migrants or apprentices; young people who are in a situation of particular difficulty due to their low levels of qualification and their backgrounds.

These courses provide a highly individualised offer to enable the recipients to enter the school and training system, or to direct them immediately towards the world of work. In fact, this vocational training includes a series of actions aimed at making the person aware of the current work context and to be prepared to tackle the steps to access the profession in the best possible way.

6. Some organisations offer a residential service for young people attending schools and vocational training centres. The boarding schools are equipped with a residential structure that allows the student to stay for the whole day and also overnight. It is an environment suitable for study in a climate of relaxed coexistence, with the young people constantly accompanied by a team of educators.

In boarding schools, the educator is of great importance: they assist and advise pupils during the hours of study and recreation; they sit at table with them and accompany them during the day. In some cases, students are offered a social and cultural formation that supports them in their daily studies. The day of the boarder is divided up between school-time, study-time and recreational, sporting and spiritual time.

7. By way of conclusion, we would like to point out that in Salesian schools and vocational training centres it is essential that all members of the educational and pastoral community share the same intentions and convictions. For this purpose, a number of priorities are needed:

• To sustain the dynamics of teaching and learning on a solid educational foundation.

- To cultivate a continuous and critical attention to cultural phenomena, the world of work and new technologies in the classroom.

- To offer a gradual and orderly pedagogical-methodological approach that encourages young people to discover their own life plan.

- To establish a social and evangelical vision of work, and to promote the proper integration of young people into the world of work as well as their continued accompaniment, maintaining regular contact with the business world.

- To guarantee the continuous updating of the professional qualifications and the Salesian identity of all of the members of the educational-pastoral community with regular formation and continuing professional development.

- To foster an appropriate pedagogy and project mentality in the field of educational action, maintaining a close relationship between educational, didactic and pastoral objectives.

4. Higher Education: An Educational and Cultural Impact on Society and the Church

The Salesian presence in this environment is today very widespread and diversified. It takes shape in academic centres under the direct responsibility of the Salesian Congregation as well as those operated in partnership with other ecclesial institutions; in colleges and residences for young university students; it is also embodied in the presence of numerous qualified Salesians with responsibility for direction, teaching, research or animation of university ministry, in Salesian, ecclesial or public institutions of higher education.

This presence is relatively new in the history of the Salesian Congregation. Although the first institution in this area dates back to 1934 (St Anthony's College, Shillong, India), the perception of the importance of this level of education and the development of the Salesian presence within it, occurred only in the final decades of the last century, with the worldwide growth of mass access of the middle and lower classes to higher education.

1. Under the name of Salesian Institutions of Higher Education (or IUS: Salesian University Institutions) there is a group of higher and tertiary

level study centres, of which the Salesian Congregation is the owner or is responsible, directly or indirectly. The differences in the social conditions and in the educational systems of the countries where the centres are represent a great diversity not only in the way they are managed, but also from the point of view of the academic degrees conferred and the type of courses offered: universities, university centres, polytechnics, colleges, faculties, institutes, higher or specialised schools.

At the origin of these structures there are various motivations: the concern to offer and guarantee a higher level of education, as a natural result of the growth of middle and high schools, known for their academic and educational excellence; the need to continue to accompany young people in the period of their lives during which they make fundamental decisions for their future, and to offer an opportunity for access to university to those who come from working-class backgrounds and from the world of work. As a whole, they reflect the conviction that, through the centres of higher education, the Salesian educational-pastoral model will be able to offer society a cultural offer of quality, enriching it with competent professionals and active citizens.

Salesian University Institutions (IUS) are defined as Christian-inspired institutions, Catholic in character and Salesian in nature. They follow the scientific and academic tradition of the university structure and offer at this level the values and spirit of the Salesian educational and charismatic heritage, thus becoming institutions of higher education with a specific identity, both within the Church and in society. As a Church community, Salesian University Institutions want to be a Christian presence in the university world in the face of the great challenges of society and culture; as a presence of the Salesian Congregation, they are characterised by the commitment to young people from the working classes, by academic communities with a clear Salesian identity, by the Christian and Salesian-oriented institutional programme and by the educational-pastoral mission.

The academic community of Salesian University Institutions, as such, has its own institutional, academic and governmental autonomy, while respecting the mission and the purpose entrusted to it by the Church and the Salesian Congregation, as well as the specific direction set out in its statutes and regulations.

The academic community is the focus of the IUS mission, as is the educational-pastoral community in other Salesian environments and works. Its members are jointly responsible for the development of a comprehensive educational programme for young people, and act responsibly to the needs and expectations of the society in which they are involved. It provides scientific, professional, humanistic, artistic and technical training at the highest level, while at the same time it is committed to the values of a healthy and balanced humanism and the Salesian charism, outlined in the institutional plan.

2. On another level, the expansion of the higher education sector in various countries, considered necessary for economic and social development and also for the consolidation of democracy, has meant increased access to higher education for young people from the middle and working classes. This has meant a growth not only in the number and type of higher education institutions, but also in the facilities and accommodation services that are essential to ensure access for young people who live far away from the centres of study.

The growing need to provide these young people with hospitality, and above all a positive experience of personal, Christian and professional growth, has encouraged Salesian communities to create various structures for welcoming young university students from abroad. In accordance with the higher education systems and socioeconomic conditions of each nation or region, colleges or university residences have been established either as separate structures close to the centres of study or as integrated structures within the campus of the IUS or institutions belonging to others.

University colleges are centres outside the university system that offer students a welcoming space and a training programme. Many colleges are the result of the response to the new needs of young people, particularly in cities where large, traditional university structures are located. In these cases, they have generally gone from an initial offer of basic accommodation to the construction of places offering personal, Christian, academic and professional formation.

The university colleges, as separate structures of the university campus, are generally associated with a Salesian work in which other environments are present (oratory-youth centre, school, parish, etc.) and in whose structure they are integrated and with which they are related.

University accommodation, on the other hand, are buildings belonging to the same higher education institution, designed to host students. They are generally located on campus and, in addition to providing accommodation and support services for living and study, they allow students to gain on-campus experience, enjoying the full range of academic services (library, study and consultation areas) and educational services (cultural, sporting, religious and social activities and programmes) provided by the institution.

In addition to the extracurricular activities on offer, the universities provide students their own programme of personal, spiritual, social and cultural formation and growth, integrating the services already available on the campus with the added value of living together and participating in a shared experience.

As Salesian educational institutions, schools and universities are called upon to promote a formation programme and offer educational and pastoral accompaniment. As this structure is designed, accompaniment should take care of personal growth towards full maturity, which implies the ability to manage one's life with autonomy and freedom; not only the appreciation of interpersonal relationships, but also of service to others; the development of responsibility for one's studies and formation; the growth of one's capacity for reflection, discussion and commitment in the search for truth; the discovery of one's vocation, and the creation of a life plan that addresses spiritual growth.

This type of presence is enriched by the educators in charge of managing the pastoral structure, as well as by the young university students who are involved, to varying degrees, in animating the life of the residence hall and achieving its objectives.

5. The Parish and the Shrine: A Place of Welcome and Hope for Working-class Young People

The particular attention to young people in the parish entrusted to the Salesians is not exclusive or discriminatory, but preferential. It is therefore a precious gift for the whole ecclesial community. This priority focus on young people offers a systematic approach to evangelisation and education, with incremental and sustained pathways of education in the faith, applicable also for the families of the area.

Don Bosco's apostolic zeal for the poorest young people of Turin led him to create a parish for young people without a parish. However, he himself accepted seven parishes in his time. In 1887 he wrote a regulation on the proper functioning of the parish. After many years, the Salesians agreed that the parish offers vast possibilities and favourable conditions for fulfilling the aims of their mission, especially in the education of young people and the poor and working class. It is a place where the educational-pastoral model has its own style.

The Salesian parish is typically characterised by being welcoming. The inclusion of evangelisation in the popular culture requires the ability to tune into the diversity of its manifestations. Evangelisation is contextualised and integrated into people's lives, taking into account their history, tradition and culture, their customs and their roots.

The parish is the community which the Church establishes first and foremost, in a well-defined sociocultural context, the mission entrusted to Her by Jesus. It constitutes a large community of the baptised, a 'section' of the universal Church; the Salesian parish is also the bearer of a charism of the Church for the Church, where it must constantly recreate its fidelity to Jesus. In other words, there is a clear and preferential commitment to the dynamism of youthful evangelisation, especially when this apostolic dimension is one of the greatest concerns and urgent challenges of the Church.

The Christian community is the historical place where communion is lived: in it, the priest, the catechist, the young person, the volunteer and those who carry out a service in the Christian community find their home. As a community of communities, the parish creates a broad fabric of human relationships, of strong bonds that foster communion and fraternity, a 'spirituality of communion'.

Engaged in dialogue with diverse cultural environments, the parish helps everyone to develop values, judgement standards and lifestyles according to the Gospel. It proclaims the Gospel and Jesus in intimate relationship with people's stories, their problems and their possibilities. Moved by the desire to heal damaged situations, the individual allows themself to be guided by the value of human fulfilment they find in God. The development of the Salesian educational-pastoral approach requires simultaneously spreading of the Gospel and assisting people. This approach, considering all pastoral action as a reflection of the Gospel, is not limited to the administration of the sacraments alone.

This environment also has a formative dimension for young people, accompanying them to a greater understanding of the faith, suggesting ideas for understanding this faith and preparing them to be witnesses of it. It also encourages the progressive involvement of young families in their children's faith education.

The parish community is encouraged to be a place of welcome and hope for the neighbourhood, especially for those who are weary, distressed, marginalised, sick and suffering. For this reason, it is essential to foster positive actions in the face of an ever-changing reality, taking care of interpersonal relationships (listening and talking) with the most needy, the sick, new neighbours, associations or groups and all those who ask for Christian services. In addition, the parish community needs to be concerned and sensitive to everything related to the world of youth, welcoming young people so that they feel 'at home'.

Therefore, in close cooperation with the established institutions of the area, the parish strongly promotes the protection and promotion of inalienable human rights, sharing their concerns and aspirations.

6. Works and Services for Young People at Risk: Addressing Vulnerability through Preventive Action

Like Don Bosco, the Salesians give an immediate and innovative response to the vulnerability of so many children and young people. With the same educational outlook, we find today so many scenarios of social exclusion in its many forms which must be combatted with effective preventive action.

Driven by the world of social exclusion that many young people suffer today, the Salesian educator recognises the need to ensure the application of Don Bosco's insights through his Preventive System. Young people at risk are a particularly vulnerable group of people that attracts the attention of every Salesian educator: each one of them has accrued in his or her life an abundance of shortcomings and failures, has his or her own particular history of absenteeism, of resistance, of missed opportunities. Consequently, young people's transition to adult life becomes a risky operation that makes them particularly vulnerable.

Poverty and exclusion are growing every day to a tragic extent: poverty that hurts individuals and communities, especially young people, to the point of becoming a structural and global reality of life. The cruelty of this vulnerability pushes and commits us to implement immediate short and medium-term responses that, by overcoming injustices and social inequalities, give young people new opportunities to define a life plan and integrate themselves responsibly into society.

1. For these young people, the Salesian educational-pastoral model is translated into a wide variety of projects, initiatives and services.[5] In these services, sometimes the intervention is to immediately respond to the primary need for survival (food, water, medical care, shelter in a family environment). This comprehensive educational service is a pedagogical accompaniment offered to young people during their development, aimed at making them autonomous individuals capable of responsibly managing their own lives. Moreover, many of these works and services present a new pedagogical and Salesian model and therefore require professional competence, specialised training and collaboration with public and religious institutions.

An overview is provided in the following list:

- Works for street children: home-schools, day centres and family homes. There are also residential facilities for homeless young people. There are centres for refugees and runaways, for street children living on the outskirts of the city, for homeless, abandoned or orphaned children.

---

5   Some of the most systematised experiences can be found in Orlando (ed.), *Con Don Bosco, educatori dei giovani del nostro tempo*, 210–332.

- Service for young people with additional needs: juveniles under protective measures for criminal responsibility; prisoners; child soldiers; children exploited by sex tourism and abuse; young people with special educational needs both physical and intellectual.

- Assistance to immigrants: literacy; psychological, pedagogical and educational support; legal advice to obtain residency status; assistance in acquiring social and professional skills; participation and integration in the community.

- Accommodation and accompaniment for the recovery and rehabilitation of drug addicts, young people with behavioural disorders, AIDS-HIV patients.

- Alternative educational services to tackle the problem of school failure: socio-educational projects; vocational and pre-vocational workshops; outreach and enrichment classes; professional workshops; training courses for the unemployed; educational catch-up programmes.

- Involvement in social and cultural activities in deprived neighbourhoods; intervention to welcome and accompany those who are victims of violence, war and religious fanaticism.

- Centres for care and support for the family in its educational role; services for young people suffering from broken homes, homelessness or inadequate housing.

- Specific services to support women: literacy, responsible motherhood, health and hygiene education.

2. As we have been saying, prevention and dealing with the possible needs of young people in every environment, in every context, not only in the works and in the specific service of attention to social exclusion, is a typical and urgent concern of a Salesian heart. In fact, in every educational-pastoral community it is necessary to respond to any form of youth distress. However, at this point we wish to underline how the personal condition of certain young people requires appropriate interventions and services for recovery and re-education, spaces where it is difficult to find linear and standardised paths.

The Salesian model's intervention is primarily educational, working on the potential resources, the evolutionary possibilities, the proactive qualities of understanding and support on the part of the educator and does not only intervene from a holistic, therapeutic or clinical point of view. At the end of the day, educating means fulfilling a life-giving mission.

In fact, the experience of the Salesian educational-pastoral model has strengthened some of Don Bosco's intuitions that must be taken into account for the consolidation of this educational undertaking. For example, as we saw earlier, the Oratory offered abandoned young people the opportunity to belong to a real family in which they could grow and prepare for life; this is why Don Bosco considered the community experience to be important. In fact, a family environment makes it possible to live relationships with positive adult influences, it strengthens horizontal and vertical links with peers and adults, it breaks down the barrier of mistrust and awakens educational interest. The community is a social space where young people learn their social relationships and also their own personal reality, where the person feels valued, where interpersonal relationships take on great importance and is a place for learning about life in society.

In this sense, Don Bosco presents a system that is among the most suitable for the re-education of young people harmed by delinquency or seriously marginalised. From his model we understand that it is necessary to exercise patience and perseverance to protect and develop the religious awakening, bringing out the positive in each young person, the awareness of their dignity, their intentional or unintentional quests, their desire for authenticity, connection, empowerment and meaning. There can be no substitutes in this task, no one can replace anyone, everyone must find the inner question for which it is worth investing one's best energies and getting personally involved.

For this reason, some specific forms of support and action that can facilitate this education of inner life are, for example: to elicit questions about the meaning of life (What is the meaning of my life? What kind of person do I want to be?); being present at celebrations and important events in their family, social and religious life; offering values that guide the religious search and encourage openness to faith; presenting the Christian humanism of the Gospel of Jesus as Good News; inviting them to feel welcomed as members of a community that loves them and accompanies them; proposing simple and meaningful religious experiences, taking on initiatives committed to social, environmental or charitable causes in general.

7. New Realities and Youth Organisations: New Forms of Presence in the Face of New Educational Contexts

The Salesian charismatic heritage has undoubtedly ensured from the outset that the educational function was not relegated to the school setting alone; the model includes other integrated and integrating contexts of non-formal education as part of the same formative project.

It is essential, then, to recognise that more and more attention is being paid to the link between schools and formal education and these non-school educational practices that have an equally decisive influence on the development, socialisation and training of individuals. In many cases, language is used which has a playful, symbolic and educational function simultaneously.

Indeed, in the Salesian world, educational activities, services or initiatives have been developed that respond to the new urgencies of young people and offer adequate responses to the demands of education with diverse, accessible and stimulating activities in general. Among these are vocational animation programmes, specialised formation and educational-pastoral animation services (volunteer opportunities, summer camps, among others), workshops or craft centres, environmental education centres (nature lessons, farm schools, interpretation centres) and leisure associations and services.

The latter include leisure time and sociocultural animation schools, alternative leisure centres, various sports group initiatives, enterprises based on music, dance, languages, theatre, or the environment (camping, summer camps, trips and walks). There are also other forms of intervention through children's libraries and play areas.

These new presences are projects rather than structures, and they respond to changing needs and urgencies, adapting with freedom of action and initiative. It should be noted that these initiatives are carried out collectively, having a positive impact on the network of relationships through fun, enjoyment, satisfaction, relaxation, personal development and participating in activities. They use communication within the young people's natural environment, regardless of the stability of a physical surrounding. Here, it is relatively easier to involve the young people themselves in the belief that the road to be travelled together is in their hands. They are therefore an expression of a new form of presence in the world of the young, and effective tools for responding to the new educational and evangelising needs.

Epilogue

Challenges For Salesian Education

In the last few years, all the educational institutions in Salesian Provinces have been making great efforts to deepen and better express the identity of the educational-pastoral model. In general, we can state that there is a good organisation, structure and implementation of the initiatives. There is an enormous variety of apostolic works and activities at the service of the mission, as well as a high degree of involvement and attention to the target groups. The widespread presence of educational offers for young people continues to be a living educational reality, full of evangelising possibilities. In the Salesian communities in 132 countries, there is a concern to present the educational-pastoral model and to translate it into meaningful experiences.

The daily work of so many educators who offer to the various environments and to the local Church real examples of generosity, creativity and complete dedication to the cause of young people is very inspiring. Their presence is a richness, especially that of those who share the same Salesian spiritual identity and mission.

Our settings are not homogeneous and compact entities, but rather complex, diverse, dynamic and interdependent landscapes. For this reason, it is not enough to show a solid charismatic and traditional base: it is necessary to face some challenges that mark the social and ecclesial reality, with the desire to faithfully serve today's young people and the Gospel.

We can condense what has been said so far with a summary of some key elements of the model which we consider to be 'strengths' or 'commitments' to be continuously nurtured and developed.

1. Reclaiming the Educational and Pastoral Focus: Young People

"Education is not the filling of a pail, but the lighting of a fire." This phrase, by the Greek philosopher Plutarch, reminds us of the beauty and, at the same time, the challenge of educating the younger generation. To speak of formation, we must first pay close attention to people; this translates into a positive and active outlook whereby the intention of every educator in the Church is the complete personal and Christian fulfilment of individuals and achieving a happy life for our children and young people.

This is the expression of a true educational awareness, which also implies feeling challenged and questioned by young people and their world, with its particular features, its expectations, its problems and its discomforts. In addition to providing a response and constructing institutions, all education should begin by giving young people a voice. They do not learn by answering questions, but by asking them.

If the Salesian approach is centred on compassion and a willingness to be in contact with young people and, therefore, encountering affectively, it is essential to nurture a degree of emotional intelligence to identify the current circumstances of young people; likewise, to redouble efforts to create new formative paths (differentiation, personalisation, life experiences).

Today more than ever, young people need to be accompanied, filling their hearts with messages of meaning, life and dreams, which are understood as a visualisation of the best outcomes for the future. The situation of children and young people is driving us to create diverse learning environments. Educating is no longer primarily the transmission and memorisation of knowledge and learning, but a quest for personal growth.

For the sons of Don Bosco, education must incorporate elements of accompaniment through personalised care, closeness and the replenishment of inner resources. It was said of Don Bosco that, while the young people were playing in the playground, he would go up to one or other of them and say a personal word ("a little word in their ear"), speaking of their present difficulties and also of their immediate and future hopes.

Thus, assistance becomes one of the key elements of Salesian pastoral accompaniment; it is the active presence of the educator as a basic principle of Salesian educational mission. The Salesian 'playground', in a broad sense, is a living representation of the educational interaction between educators and students. Salesian pedagogy has adopted the wise awareness that those who educate cannot be absent from the environments where young people make their decisions and condition their opinions, which are not always understandable in the eyes of adults. This is why it is a priority for the Preventive System that young people have educators with the soul of a playground, not only busy with planning and organising, but also willing to 'waste time' with them.

2. The Most Needy Require a Comprehensive Training Programme

The poorest and most needy are the priority focus of Salesian educational and pastoral action. Attention to them, the working class and the world of work are the genetic code of Don Bosco's system. Salesian activities are available to those who are most in need; an educational programme is offered to those who do not have access to education, and an attempt is made to respond to the challenge posed by the new forms of poverty that afflict children and young people. This requires a unified and unifying project (the educational-pastoral approach) attentive to the integral formative aspect that especially helps the most vulnerable to develop all their possibilities and resources.

When we speak of 'new poverties', it seems reasonable to think of some current issues that are particularly challenging, some that are creating areas of poverty on a personal and institutional level. The issue of exclusion and its correlation with poverty brings with it certain consequences: the issue of disconnected emotional affiliation in the couple, sexuality and the family; youth unemployment; religious apathy and the lack of a prophetic spirit in consumer societies; social inequality, which causes spiritual and material misery (hunger and illiteracy). To this we must add the emergence of a series of social risk scenarios for young people: domestic violence, gender based violence among peers, the danger of ICT and Internet abuse and addiction. Faced with these realities that challenge us, Paul VI said, at the end of the Second Vatican Council, that the Church has placed herself at the side of suffering humanity, assuring everyone: "Know that you are not alone, separated, abandoned or useless."[1] This sums up very well our mission as educators in the face of young people and their poverty.

We find throughout this text good reason to believe that the Salesian educational-pastoral model can situate itself on the current level of wounded humanity and to continue to offer it the healing balm of the Gospel. This is very much in line with the directions of Pope Francis, who invites us to seek a profound renewal of spiritual experience, underlining the importance of mercy and encouraging all members of the Church to venture out without fear an open dialogue with the world. A church rather than a customs-house; a table rather than a podium; a pathway rather than a cul-de-sac.

---

1   Pope Paul VI, *Address to the Poor, the Sick and the Suffering*, (December 8, 1965).

3. Co-responsibility, a Fad or a Sign?

The climate of co-responsibility in an educational establishment has a high educational value; and this is built up by everyone, based on the willingness of consecrated and lay people. Co-responsibility makes it possible to share the charism and the Salesian mission. For this reason, every Salesian centre must foster environments of real participation, mutual help and support. We can say that co-responsibility is one of the best ways to give shape to the authentic Salesian style.

The goal of the educational-pastoral model is to help young people to articulate the complexity of their lives, adopting a humane and humanising style; and all this is possible if there are groups sharing responsibility. But this option has many implications; it is a question of a qualified commitment, not a simple development of activities or services.

Sometimes, after a few years, some educators who began their commitment in an enthusiastic way, find themselves overwhelmed, lacking in resources and educational passion, with little motivation to continue to assume their responsibilities and to be part of projects that do not excite them. To avoid these circumstances, it is necessary to continue to form and enrich each other, religious and laity, sharing the same agenda of values, discovering affectively and intellectually the charism with different levels of depth and experience. There is a high cost associated with dispensing with personal formation in the educational-pastoral approach. Experience tells us that this joint formation is not a prelude to the community's response to the mission, but rather a support for the journey that is travelled as an educational-pastoral community.

The shared mission between religious and lay people is not limited to collaborating in educational tasks, but goes as far as co-responsibility, which implies participating in the same educational passion, sharing information and decisions, actively intervening in the processes of drawing up and evaluating educational initiatives and assuming responsibilities based on the competencies and possibilities of each individual. To respond to the challenges that education and evangelisation pose for us today, we need a great openness of mind and the capacity for overcoming patterns of relationships and governance that may have served in the past, but that no longer respond to the needs of the present time.

It is therefore necessary to rely on a culture of consensus and agreement, of responsible participation, where everyone contributes their best to achieve a joint undertaking that is always felt to be their own.

In this way the dynamic interaction between consecrated and lay people becomes urgent. Those who offer different contributions and degrees of involvement in the development of the same 'community' educational-pastoral programme are more important than a mere distribution of tasks. Its practical application makes it, with the passage of time, a true sign of sharing spirituality, style and mission.

4. A Model Cannot be Understood Without a Network

We continue to believe that the Salesian educational-pastoral model and its implementation in a project are at the heart of institutions, and that this fact can be translated into multiple contexts. However, it must be stated with equal intensity that without an effective membership of the institutional network, without a culture of coexistence, its identity tends to become blurred and, finally, disappear. The model proposed here is part of the Salesian tradition and origins, and therefore plays a part in the mission of evangelisation and social development that we have described.

It is absolutely essential to broaden this perspective: few new educational issues are confined to geographical boundaries any longer. The concept of belonging to a network has enormous educational potential: the dynamics of interrelationships forces people to become involved in meeting spaces, thus offering greater educational effectiveness and profitability; it stimulates the creation of permanent places for reflection in which to think about problems in a new and creative way, with practical and feasible actions; it suggests identifying opportunities that support and strengthen the meaning and direction of the educational task, especially in relatively adverse areas. In short, we are talking about changing mindsets. It is not about making differences more evident, but about ensuring the strengthening of a relationship with other institutions that live the same educational and evangelising identity.

Moreover, the educational model envisages a series of ideas that give shape to a way of proceeding in Salesian institutions. The culmination is to come to think that these ideas, with their charismatic traits, must not only exist in one context, but also bring together the educational-pastoral communities and those who are outside, those others who are external collaborators (people, institutions, organisations), in a project capable of uniting them in the development of their mission. This is a significant turning point, an antidote that invites us to get away from the cultural individualism of those who persist with the same mantra: nothing good can come from anyone other than me.

If we look at the matter carefully, we can fall into the temptation of making educational approaches 'liquid',[2] to use Bauman's expression, that is, accommodating ourselves to our own environmental or cultural circumstances without sufficient perspective and criticism. The Polish sociologist defines reality as liquid because it adapts to the environment; water takes on the form of a glass, not because it has that form, but because the container gives it that form. From this approach, the need for collaboration, coordination and networking is becoming more and more pressing.

5. Urgently Needed Family Integration

To begin with, it is important to remember that the family is the first environment and fundamental reference point in a person's life, it is a key element in their socialisation, and at the same time defines their identity and the way in which they live. For this reason, it is both the goal and the subject of the educational and evangelising action of Salesian work.

It should also be said that the involvement and contribution of the family in educational work must be sought, overcoming what could be described as parental apathy, indifference or ineffective participation. In certain aspects it will be necessary to change the culture or dynamics of real and effective participation of the establishment so that it places not only the young people

---

2   Z. Bauman, *Liquid Modernity*, (Cambridge: Polity Press, 2000).

(the fundamental reason for the educational-pastoral model), but also their families at the centre of attention. Many of the misunderstandings presented by families in the different aspects of their children's education could be avoided if there were real parental involvement in the educational project itself, moving from top-down approach to more flexible and mixed ones.

On the other hand, the individualised and personal attention given to the young people makes the families see that the Salesian educational presence aims to make their children feel loved and respected as individuals. This also helps to build an educational understanding of families: to know how they live their dreams, their feelings, their contradictions, in order to relate to them and accompany them appropriately. Our education model prefers the personalisation of affective bonds, the variety of approaches, the fostering of individual abilities, the motivation to do one's own duty and the search for truth; these are not only guidelines for young people: it is also a challenge for the growth of families.

It is also important to be aware of the great variety of family models, which calls for a review of the roles of families. In this sense, we consider it especially relevant to reflect on the new concept of family from the ethical, psychological, sociological and anthropological point of view, and the challenges that this situation presents to our evangelising action; the Salesian educational system allows us to give time and space to accompany parents in their educational task, shaping boundaries and values; helping parents acquire resources and cognitive and emotional skills that guide them to respond to and navigate through the ever-changing world of youth.

Finally, it is advisable to develop more specific multi-disciplinary family care opportunities, care centres with targeted support programmes for children with various problems which can respond to complex processes requiring specialised intervention.

6. Proclaiming the Gospel through Quality Education and Pastoral Care

A reading of present-day societies shows us that the dominant culture exerts an influence on young people (and not only young people) that we might call 'seduction'. Some societal attitudes are not the result of a direct and reasoned comparison of criteria, values and attitudes, but of a constant questioning of Christian humanism. At this point, in many contexts where the Salesian educational-pastoral model is implemented, young people are faced with the choice of having to 'swim against the tide', forced to find their daily reason for hope. Many young people suffer from the pressure of wanting to live as Christians and the practical difficulty of making this choice compatible with the demands of society.

In this regard, we would like to dwell in particular on the necessity of focusing on an educational proposal with a high level of pastoral intent. The Gospel of Jesus, the Good News, is the irreplaceable realm in which our educational-pastoral model is situated. This is offered as that comprehensive and gradual formation that prepares for life and gives it ultimate and definitive meaning, while at the same time it tends to shape the learner's relationship with themselves, with others, with the world and with God.

To proclaim the Gospel explicitly and to seek to live in conformity with it is a great challenge that we must embrace. The invitation of Jesus and the mission entrusted to us undoubtedly brings positive meaning to the lives of young people, unifying and completing their characters. The educational-pastoral action has to help them to be able to direct their lives in such a way that they can feel happy and blessed. The Salesian approach is not just a programme of activities, it is a personal and loving encounter open to the unexpected God. We should encourage young people to ask themselves these two questions: What experience do I have of God? Who is Jesus for me? This is, of course, the fundamental question. If the initial conversion to the Lord has not taken place, there is no point in trying to direct one's life as a disciple. As in friendship, if the relationship is not nurtured and nourished, it will eventually die. If the dialogue between the Lord, who calls, and the believer's trusting response is not continually repeated and renewed, it will tend to become stagnant.

Therefore, the processes of pastoral animation cannot be without a good structuring of spirituality. The lack of a well-defined spirituality on the part of educators can obscure for many young people the dimension of the enormous gift that our message has for their lives. Every educational-pastoral community requires an authentic catechetical pedagogy, i.e. a period of spiritual learning assisted by the presence and guidance of an educational accompaniment.

We are called to carry out a contextualised evangelisation, to make sure that everything related to God can interact with what every young person is, with what forms a part of their context: their vocabulary, their way of expressing love, pain, friendship... to transmit the message of Jesus through signs and words that reach into their culture and create an experience of encounter.

7. Educators Who Take Lifelong Learning Seriously

One of the certainties that emerges from the reflections and conclusions of this book is the importance of taking advantage of every opportunity for lifelong learning and indeed of any learning opportunity. Whereas in the past the time for education was limited to school and higher education, today the educator is called to develop an attitude of continuous learning, an updating that lasts throughout life (lifelong learning). But this reality must come about through a crystallisation of processes, not simply as the fruit of one-off or sporadic initiatives. A successful format, among others, is the strengthening of collaborative groups, learning communities, research projects or exchanges of ideas or experiences.

This formative attitude implies having a great capacity for openness and being available for a continuous process of change and growth, without claiming to have a monopoly on a little knowledge that lasts a lifetime. In fact, regression or stagnation is a great danger for anyone involved in education. Without real openness, educationalists close themselves off in their own generational context and in nostalgia (bewilderment or disconcertment) for supposedly better times, which shows that they neither understand young people nor take on board the transformative energy of today's world. We need to remind ourselves that an educator who is up to date plays a decisive role, for this makes their offer credible and attractive. In order to adapt the educator to current times, he or she must be equipped with an internalised value system expressed in intelligible parameters.

In the absence of renewed models of reference adapted to each historical context, it is very difficult to create educational trust. The fact that there may be young people who are not in tune with their educators is a tragedy for both parties. In reality, the educational 'models' in our Salesian approach are not meant to be imitated, but rather to empower young people, who have to discover their own way of life, to freely organise their choices, to be more open to what is new without being burdened by past decisions.

8. An Education that Creates Good Citizens

Salesian education aims to awaken in children and young people an awareness of living in society, of the need to go beyond their own individual reality, of the collective sharing of the commitment to a more just world in the light of the Gospel. Citizenship implies an element realism and a touch of utopia at the same time. Utopia is not something daring and unattainable, however difficult its realisation may be. The Salesian mission, like society itself, can be and is a space for interpersonal relationships in order to build a culture of coexistence. This leads us to think that all formation for citizenship must educate towards respect and tolerance.

The validity of the Salesian pastoral model of education should not be a reason for complacency. We are called to belong to and to feel that we are an open Church, to continue to speak, listen and discuss the great problems that affect the world today: life and the family as fundamental social goods, those peoples affected by religious or civil persecution, the challenge of immigration, consumerism, which does not respect deeper desires; the concern about the suffering caused by the serious economic, social and moral crisis that has affected so many societies, and so on. Catholic educational institutions must respond with directness and closeness, a palpable sign of the church coming out of its buildings and making the foyer and its entrance area larger and more welcoming.

As can be seen in these pages, the Salesian model prepares young people for living together in an increasingly pluralistic society. The tutoring, personal accompaniment, education in values, the education of conscience, education for living together and participating, the dynamics born of the commitment to faith education, cooperation and charitable projects, are all initiatives that strengthen Don Bosco's happy intuition: to educate "honest citizens".

In this commitment to civil society, we must respond to a quality education that involves educating for citizenship through the curriculum and educational programmes in order to involve ourselves educationally in the construction of a more respectful coexistence. We cannot lose sight of the fact that the Salesian model seeks an education with broad horizons and lofty goals, and that this added quality involves, in the pastoral educational project, not subordinating the values of the culture of peace, democracy, sustainable development, equity, solidarity and justice to the economy or profitability that are detrimental to human dignity.

The cultural mission of education is to help to understand, preserve, strengthen, promote and disseminate national, regional and international cultures in a varied and diverse context. It is essential to grasp the emerging dynamics of our time, and also to grasp their impact on people's lives and on their formation. In fact, in Salesian centres different cultural and religious traditions coexist, peoples and nations come together. The educational-pastoral community is a melting pot of different cultures and intercultural encounters in which an openness to difference and a critical appreciation of other cultures, experiences and beliefs, should be fostered. In the Salesian model, educational environments must be a bridge between people, cultures and civilisations. The major challenge of Salesian education is that of offering in a place of encounter diligently achieved and mastered values of solidarity.

We are aware that many themes have been suggested in this text and that they deserve a separate reflection in order to give each one the appropriate consideration. The main goal of this work, however, rests on the idea of specifying the conditions that make the Salesian educational-pastoral model possible. At the end of the book, we would like to recall that the essence of the Salesian educational model is not written in these pages, but it always has a face: that of young people.

Appendix 1

Chronology of Don Bosco, His Place and His Time

The 'Preparation' (1815–1844): Formative Years

1815 (August 16). Born in the village of Becchi, in the municipality of Castelnuovo d'Asti (today Castelnuovo Don Bosco).

1817. His father dies. At the age of twenty-nine, his mother, Mamma Margaret, has to take care of her three children: Antony (son of a previous marriage), Joseph and John.

1824. Despite the opposition of his half-brother Antony, he was introduced to reading and writing by a priest, Don Giuseppe Lacquer.

1826 (at Easter). He is admitted to his first communion. The following year, he was a farm hand on the Moglia farm (until December 1828).

1829. He returned to the study of Italian and Latin with the 74-year-old priest Don Giovanni Calosso.

1830. He attends the communal primary school in Castelnuovo (Christmas 1830 to summer 1831), while staying with a tailor.

1831. From November he is a student at the Chieri public school of Grammar, Humanities and Rhetoric. With his companions he organises the 'Society of Joy' (until 1835).

1835. He enters the Seminary of Chieri, where he studies philosophy and theology, with the financial help of some fellow villagers.

1841. On June 5, he is ordained to the priesthood in Turin and arrives there in November from his home village. He enters the priestly residence, the *Convitto Ecclesiastico di San Francesco di Assisi*, for pastoral training: practical study of morals and homiletics; at the same time, he begins to gather and give catechesis to boys and adults. During the three years he remained at the *Convitto* (1841–1844), due to various favourable circumstances and personal inclinations, he would feel more and more committed to the problems of the 'poor and abandoned' youth. On December 8, he met Bartholomew Garelli and began his pastoral work with the poorest boys from outside the city.

1844. He is chaplain in one of the institutions of the Marchioness of Barolo. In the two-year period 1844–1846 he would bring his oratorical vocation to a decisive maturity, and he would gather more and more boys; with his tenacious perseverance he would find a definitive place for his emblematic work: the Oratory.

The Fundamental Features of his Educational Activity (1845–1870): The Key Years of Change, The Direction of the Salesian Work and its Growth Outside Turin

1845 (May)–**1846** (March). The difficult pilgrimages of the 'Oratory' from San Pietro in Vincoli to the Dora Mills, Moretta House and Filippi Meadow take place. The *Storia ecclesiastica* is published for the use of the schools.

1846 (April). The Oratory is definitively established in the Pinardi house, in the outlying area of Valdocco, where in November he goes to live with his mother; during the winter he begins evening classes teaching reading and writing, and later drawing and arithmetic. Don Bosco comes into regular contact with the *La Generala* correctional school for four years.

1847. A small orphanage was established in the Oratory of St Francis de Sales. Meanwhile, this first oratory was joined by another—the Oratory of St Aloysius—in a crucial part of the city: Porta Nuova. Here the Company of St Aloysius is founded. *Il giovane provveduto* ('The Companion of Youth) and *Storia sacra* ('Sacred History') are published.

1848. He begins the publication of *L'Amico della Gioventù. Giornale religioso, morale e politico (*it will last eight months, later merging with the *Istruttore del Popolo)* and the *Sistema metrico decimale*.

1849. He takes over the management of a third oratory—the Guardian

Angel—and founds the *Società degli Operi o de Mutuo Soccorso* (Workers' or Mutual Aid Society).

1851. Thanks to public and private subsidies he acquires the Pinardi house as owner and begins to buy land and buildings to enlarge the oratorian work.

1852 (March 31). Archbishop Fransoni of Turin appoints Don Bosco 'spiritual chief-director' of the Oratories of St Francis de Sales, St Aloysius and the Guardian Angel.

1853. He begins the publication of the *Letture cattoliche* and opens an in house workshop for shoemakers and tailors.

1854. In Don Bosco's mind, the idea of a religious society dedicated to the mission of the youth was beginning to take shape. For this reason, he proposes to two clerics—among whom is Michael Rua—and two young men—one of them, John Cagliero—to experiment with a form of religious association, the seed of the future Salesian Society. First discussions with the minister Urbano Ratazzi, in which he speaks about the validity of the Preventive System. Dominic Savio (1842–1857) is one of Valdocco's pupils. Bookbinders' workshop.

1855. The Third Internal Elementary, today we say the Secondary School, is established (up to now the young students have attended public schools). He writes the *Storia d'Italia*.

1856. The carpentry workshops are opened and the first and second elementary classes are introduced. Foundation of the 'Company of the Immaculate Conception'.

1857. The 'Company of the Blessed Sacrament' is founded and the Piccolo Clero is constituted; a Youth Conference of St Vincent de Paul is also established.

1858. He made his first trip to Rome to submit to Pius IX his proposal for a religious society consecrated to the young and the first draft of the *Constitutions*. He had 320 members in Valdocco.

1859. A first group commits itself with a solemn promise in anticipation of the vows: the *Società Salesiana* is born. As far as the State was concerned, it was a private association of citizens; it began the arduous process of obtaining ecclesiastical approval. The elementary cycle is completed (five classes of secondary school). The 'Society of St Joseph' is founded, and the 'Life of Dominic Savio' is published.

1860. The first lay people (coadjutors) were present in the privately constituted religious society.

1861. The typographers' workshop and press are established. Don Bosco has 600 boarders and publishes the 'Life of Miguel Magone'.

1862. Mechanical workshop. Profession of religious vows of the first Salesians (May 14).

1863. The first building site outside Turin is inaugurated in Mirabello Monferrato, under the direction of Don Rua. The construction of the church of Maria Ausiliatrice begins. Publishes a new edition of *Il giovane provveduto* and writes the *Memoirs of the Oratory*.

1864. The municipal college of Lanzo Torinese, second house in Turin, begins its activity; it receives the recognition of the Holy See, *Decretum laudis, in* favour of the Salesian Society.

1865. Draft of the *Biblioteca degli scrittori latini,* to be published the following year under the title *Selecta ex latinis scriptoribus in usum scholarum*. Don Bosco has 700 boarders and 48 Salesians.

1868. Consecration of the Church of Mary Help of Christians.

1869. Pontifical approval of the Salesian Society. The first volume of the *Biblioteca della Gioventù Italiana* is published (in 1885 it will reach the 204th and final edition).

1870. Founding of the municipal college-residence of Alassio (the first college outside Piedmont).

Organisational and 'Theoretical' Consolidation of the Congregation's Institutions and National, European and South American Development (1871–1888)

1871. Founding of the apprentice school in Marassi (Genoa), which moves the following year to Sampierdarena (Genoa). He publishes the fourth improved edition of the *Storia ecclesiastica*. He opens the elementary day schools in Valdocco.

1872. Acceptance into the College of Nobles of Valsalice (Turin). Foundation of the Congregation of the Daughters of Mary Help of

Christians, a religious congregation for women, under the title of the Institute of the Daughters of Mary Help of Christians.

1874. The *Constitutions of the Salesian Society* are definitively approved by the Holy See. Publishes *Cenno istorico sulla Congregazione di San Francesco di Sales.*

1875. The works of Don Bosco begin to spread in Europe (France, Spain, England) and on the South American continent (Argentina, Uruguay, Brazil, etc.), with educational, scholastic and professional institutes, initiatives for the care of emigrants and missionary activities.

1876. Definitive approval of the Association of Salesian Cooperators. Tenth edition of the *Storia sacra.*

1877. The first General Chapter of the Society of St Francis de Sales is celebrated, followed, during Don Bosco's lifetime, by three others: 1880, 1883 and 1886. In 1877, the classic pages on the Preventive System and the *Regulations* of the Oratory of St Francis de Sales for boarders were published. Likewise, the *Regulations* for the houses. In August, the *Bollettino Salesiano* begins.

1880. Don Bosco agrees to build the church of the Sacred Heart in Rome (it is inaugurated seven years later).

1881. The Salesians enter Spain (Utrera).

1883. Triumphal journey to Paris. The *Letter on punishments* dates from this date.

1884. Penultimate trip to Rome (the nineteenth) because of problems related to the construction of the Sacred Heart Church and the obtaining of special juridical guarantees for his religious society. May 10: *Letter from Rome.*

1886 (April 8–May 6). Exceptional reception and stay in Spain (Barcelona).

1888 (January 31). Death of Don Bosco.

Appendix 2

Brief Bibliography of Don Bosco the Educator

Suggested references to some sources and studies considered particularly suitable to introduce Don Bosco as an educator.

Bibliographies

Diekmann, H. *Bibliografia generale di Don Bosco. Deutschsprachige Don-Bosco-Literatur, 1883–1994.* Rome: LAS, 1997.

Gianotti, S. (ed.). *Bibliografia generale di Don Bosco. I. Bibliografia italiana, 1844–1992.* Rome: LAS, 1995, 11–99.

González, G. *Bibliografía de Don Bosco y otros temas salesianos (1877–2007).* Rome: Aragne, 2008.

Schepens, J. *Bibliografia generale di Don Bosco. Bibliographie française, 1853–2006. Nederlandstalige bibliografie, 1883–2006.* Rome: LAS, 2007 (also in *RSS* 26 [2007], 113–333).

Stella, P. *Don Bosco: Life and Work*, tr. by John Drury. New Rochelle, New York: Don Bosco Publications, 1985.

_____. *Don Bosco: Religious Outlook and Spirituality*, tr. by John Drury. New Rochelle, NY: Salesiana Publishers, 1996.

Don Bosco's Publications

Letter of John Bosco to Don Giacomo Costamagna (August 10, 1885), in the Salesian Historical Institute, *Sources Salesians. Don Bosco and his work (anthological collection)*. Madrid: CCS, 2015, 410–411.

John Bosco's Letter from Rome (1884), in Salesian Historical Institute, *Salesian Sources*, 402–408.

Constitutions of the Society of St Francis of Sales [1858]–1875. [3rd ed.]. Rome: Editrice SDB, 2015.

Epistolario. Introduction, critical texts and notes edited by F. Motto. Rome: LAS, 1991–2016, 6 vols.

Introduction to the Plan of Regulations for the Male Oratory of St Francis de Sales (1854), by John Bosco, in P. Braido (ed.), *Juan Bosco, el arte de educar: escritos y testimonios*. With the collaboration of J. M. Prellezo García / A. da Silva Ferreira. Madrid: CCS, 1994.

El joven instruido en la práctica de sus deberes en los ejercicios de la piedad cristiana (1847), by John Bosco, in Instituto Histórico Salesiano, *Fuentes salesianas*, 551–613.

Memoirs of the Oratory of St Francis de Sales from 1815 to 1855, tr. D. Lyons, with notes and commentary by E. Ceria. L. Castelvecchi and M. Mendl. New Rochelle, NY: Don Bosco Publications, 1989.

Edited works. Prima serie: *Libri e opuscoli*. Rome: LAS, 1976–1977, 37 vols.; Seconda serie: *Contributi su giornali e periodici*, vol. 38. Rome: LAS, 1987 [this is an anastatic reprint of all the printed texts of Don Bosco, with the exception of programmes, testimonies, leaflets, posters. The circulars and requests for help are included in the editions of his epistolary].

The Preventive System in the education of youth (1877), by John Bosco, in Salesian Historical Institute, *Salesian Sources*. 392–399.

Life of the young saint Dominic Savio, pupil of the Oratory of St Francis de Sales, in John Bosco, *Lives of young people: the biographies of Dominic Savio, Michael Magone and Francis Besucco*. Introductory essay and historical notes by A. Giraudo. Madrid: CCS, 2012

Biographies of Don Bosco with Extensive Bibliography

Braido P. *Don Bosco, Priest of the Young in the Century of Freedoms.* Rosario: Didascalia, 2009 (original ed. *Don Bosco, prete dei giovani nel secolo delle libertà.* Rome: LAS, 2003.

Desramaut, F. *Don Bosco en son temps (1815-1888).* Turin: SEI, 1996.

Lenti, A. J. *Don Bosco: History and Spirit.* Edited by Aldo Giraudo; seven volumes. Rome: LAS, 2007-2010.

Essays and Studies on Salesian Education

Acosta, F. 'Las "buenas noches" en el marco del Proyecto Educativo Pastoral Salesiano', in *Misión Joven* 78-79 (1983), 21-34.

Avanzini, G. 'The pedagogy of St John Bosco in his own life', *Don Bosco in History: Proceedings of the First International Congress of Studies on Saint John Bosco, Pontifical Salesian University - Rome, January 16-20, 1989,* Online: https://www.sdb.org/en/ Don_Bosco/Biographical_Material/Documents/Don_Bosco_en_la_ Historia_UPS_1989 [Accessed 20/06/2022].

Barbera, M. 'La pedagogía de san Juan Bosco', in P. Stella, *San Juan Bosco en la historia de la educación.* Madrid: CCS, 1996, 91-110.

Bellerate, B. 'Don Bosco and the humanist school', in *Don Bosco in history,* 317-332.

Bongioanni, M. *Don Bosco y el teatro.* Madrid: CCS, 1991.

Bracco, G. 'Don Bosco and civil society' in *Don Bosco in history,* 231-236.

Braido, P. *Breve historia del 'Sistema Preventivo',* Rome: LAS, 1993.

_____. *Don Bosco al alcance de la mano,* Madrid: CCS, 1993.

_____. *La experiencia pedagógica de Don Bosco,* Rome: LAS, 1988.

_____. *Juan Bosco. El arte de educar: escritos y testimonios,* Madrid: CCS, 1994.

_____. *Prevenir, no reprimir: el sistema educativo de Don Bosco,* Madrid: CCS, 2002.

_____. *El sistema educativo de Don Bosco,* Madrid: CCS, 1984.

Cian, L. *El sistema educativo de Don Bosco y las líneas maestras de su estilo*, Madrid: CCS, 1987.

Ceria, E. and Borgatello, D. *Biographical Memoirs of St John Bosco*. (New Rochelle, NY: Salesiana Publishers, 1983vol. XIII, 480. (original: *Memorie biografiche di Don Bosco*, 19 vols. Turin: San Benigno Canavese, I-IX [1898–1917], by G. B. Lemoyne; X [1939], by A. Amadei; XI- XIX [1930–1939], by E. Ceria).

Delgado, B. 'Don Bosco, pedagogue of joy', in *Don Bosco in history*, 505–513.

Gallego Gago, U. M. *El tiempo libre en el sistema educativo de Don Bosco*. Madrid: Complutense University, 1987.

Jiménez, F. *El amor supera al reglamento. Educational practice and theory in Don Bosco*. Madrid: CCS, 2003.

Stella, P. *San Juan Bosco en la historia de la educación*. Madrid: CCS, 1995.